WHY SHOULD I GO TO BARCELONA

WHY SHOULD I GO TO ↴

BARCELONA

THE CITY YOU DEFINITELY NEED TO
VISIT BEFORE YOU TURN 30 (OR 130)

THIS IS WHY!

Barcelona effortlessly combines Mediterranean vibes with architectural beauty. Gaudí's masterpieces, like the awe-inspiring Sagrada Família and Park Güell, speak to the imagination. Barcelona is a vibrant city full of culture, tradition, design, beach life, and breathtaking coastal views. From the lively Barceloneta Beach to the more relaxed Bogatell Beach, there's a spot for everyone to soak up the sun and enjoy the Mediterranean Sea.

We love the city's dynamic street life and its bustling markets that offer an authentic taste of Catalan gastronomy. Whether you're enjoying tapas, sipping a refreshing *horchata*, or dipping your *churros* in hot chocolate, your taste buds are in for a treat. Barcelona's nightlife is legendary, with a wide range of bars, clubs, and music venues catering to every taste and budget. Dance the night away at one of the many beach clubs, enjoy some live music in El Gòtic, or make your way to trendy bars in El Born and L'Eixample.

Exploring Barcelona is easy and affordable. Walk through the charming narrow streets of the historic centre, rent a bike to explore further out, or use the efficient metro system. Join a free walking tour to get to know the city's rich history and visit viewpoints like the Bunkers and Tibidabo for some spectacular panoramic views. Each area has its own charm, from the bohemian vibes of Gràcia and the creativity of Poblenou to the elegance of L'Eixample. One thing is certain: your first visit to Barcelona won't be your last.

CONTENTS

DISTRICTS

Barcelona is divided into ten districts, each consisting of several neighbourhoods. When you're looking for an address within the L'Eixample district, the Gran Via or the Avinguda Diagonal, it's advisable to look up the specific intersection, as the streets in this area are very long. We list the coolest districts and areas below.

El Gòtic (Gothic Quarter)

Barcelona's rich history is present everywhere in El Gòtic. Nestled between the bustling La Rambla and the vibrant waterfront, this century-old neighbourhood weaves a labyrinth of narrow streets and historic buildings. From the majestic Gothic Cathedral to the atmospheric Plaça Reial, every corner narrates a tale of the city's past.

SPAIN
GRACIA
POBLENOU
L'EIXAMPLE
EL BORN
EL GÒTIC
LA BARCELONETA
EL RAVAL
SANT ANTONI

El Born

El Born is nestled between Ciutadella Park and El Gòtic. This neighbourhood is also part of Ciutat Vella, the Old Town, and was the beating heart of medieval Barcelona. Today, its alleys are lined with trendy boutiques, artisanal cafés, and hidden squares with exquisite restaurants waiting to be discovered. Taking a stroll through El Born on a Saturday afternoon is one of our favourite activities.

El Raval

Discover the cultural melting pot of El Raval, nestled between historic El Gòtic and the popular residential area of El Poble-sec. Dating back to medieval times, this eclectic district is a haven for immigrants, artists, musicians, and free spirits. Visit the beautiful century-old hospital or the avant-garde museum MACBA and the lively La Boqueria market.

L'Eixample

Marvel at the architectural wonders of L'Eixample. Barcelona's iconic grid-like district was designed in the 19th century by pioneering urban planner Ildefons Cerdà. L'Eixample is characterised by its wide boulevards, elegant squares, and iconic Modernista buildings. Highlights like the Sagrada Família, Casa Milà, and Casa Batlló make it a must-visit destination.

Poblenou

Located on the northeastern edge of the city, Poblenou was once a bustling industrial district known for its factories and warehouses. Over the last decades, it has been transformed into a thriving hub for artists, designers, and tech startups. Its wide boulevards and converted warehouses now house galleries, co-working spaces, and trendy cafés.

Gràcia

Gràcia is a lively neighbourhood that was once a village on the outskirts of Barcelona. Its slim streets and lively squares are lined with cafés, boutiques, and artisan workshops. From the lively Plaça del Sol to the tranquil Plaça de la Vila de Gràcia, this charming district offers a welcome respite from the hustle and bustle of the rest of the city.

La Barceloneta

Barcelona's most popular seaside neighbourhood, located between the Old Port and El Born, is called La Barceloneta. Originally built as a fishing village in the 18th century, La Barceloneta retains its maritime charm combined with its sandy beaches, bustling promenade, and lively beach bars known as *chiringuitos*.

Sant Antoni

Named after the iconic Sant Antoni Market, Sant Antoni is part of the bustling L'Eixample district. We love this lively part of town because of its local market and fantastic eateries, especially on foodie street Carrer del Parlament. Sant Antoni is the perfect place to savour the flavours of Barcelona's culinary scene.

PRACTICAL INFO

TRAVEL

Exploring Barcelona is best done on foot, just like the locals do. The wide pavements and pedestrian-friendly streets make walking a pleasure, allowing you to stop at any café, shop, or landmark that catches your eye. However, if you are short on time or want to cover more ground, there are other options.

Barcelona's efficient public transport system includes the metro, buses, and trams, making it easy to travel the city and its surroundings in a user-friendly and affordable way. You can purchase tickets, which need to be validated before boarding, at vending machines at stations or kiosks and tobacconists. The T-Casual ticket is perfect for short stays, as it offers ten rides at a discount. The metropolitan area of Barcelona is divided into different fare zones, but most tourist attractions and central areas fall within Zone 1.

The metro is particularly convenient, covering all major areas. M signs mark the stations. The rail network FGC is another excellent option, especially if you're looking to travel to nearby destinations. FGC lines connect Barcelona with suburban areas and towns such as Terrassa and Sabadell. They also provide access to some popular attractions located outside the city, like the Montserrat mountain and monastery. Barcelona also offers an extensive network of buses, with regular services. You can buy a single ticket on the bus, or pay with a contactless debit card or mobile payment. The Nitbus operates throughout the night, ensuring you can get around even after a late night out.

DUNKIN'

For a scenic route through the city, the Bus Turístic takes you to many of Barcelona's top attractions.

Cycling is another great way to see Barcelona. The city has a network of bike lanes, and you'll find numerous bike-sharing services. Bicing is for locals only, but companies such as Donkey Republic offer their service to tourists as well. At rental shops such as Green Bikes, Mattia 46, or El Ciclo, you can also rent a bicycle affordably. If you prefer someone to show you around, choose one of many guided bike tours.

For a faster and more flexible option, consider renting a scooter. Companies like Cooltra and Acciona offer scooter rentals that are perfect for zipping through the city's traffic. Sharing a scooter is prohibited by law.

If you are looking to travel beyond Barcelona, the main train station, Estació de Sants, is your gateway. It's a major hub with connections to other Spanish cities like Madrid and Valencia, as well as international destinations like Paris. If you're arriving at or departing from Estació de Sants, the metro and various bus lines will take you directly into the heart of the city.

Taxis in Barcelona are affordable and stand out with their yellow and black colouring. There are many taxi stands, but you can also hail them. Look for the green lights on top: if it is on, the taxi is available.

P

WHERE TO STAY

Kabul

Plaça Reial 17, 08002 El Gòtic, kabul.es

This place isn't for you if you're not in Barcelona to party! This hostel is located on one of the well-known party squares: Plaça Reial. The hostel regularly hosts pub crawls and has a large rooftop terrace where you can enjoy pre-drinks, or relax during the day. Battle your hangover the day after with the free breakfast buffet. The hostel offers free city tours that you can join to learn about the cultural side of Barcelona as well.

Hostal Mare Nostrum

Carrer de Sant Pau 2, 08029 El Raval, hostalmarenostrum.com

An independent budget hotel in the heart of Barcelona. There are no tricks or gimmicks: this hotel is small, does not have a pool, but they love providing personalised service. The rooms offer space for up to four people and all of them have private bathrooms.

numa | Roca Rooms & Apartments

Carrer de Girona 81, 08009 L'Eixample, retrome-guest-house.costadebarcelona.net

Centrally located, basic, simple, and with a fun retro touch. This small hotel has fifteen rooms for up to two people. The vintage details include some original Modernista tiled floors. From Retrome you can easily walk towards highlights such as the Passeig de Gràcia.

Black Swan Hostel

Carrer Ali Bei 15, 08010 L'Eixample, hotelesfind.com/black-swan-hostel-barcelona

At this hostel, you'll find yourself in L'Eixample but very close to El Born, one of our favourite neighbourhoods and part of the lively Old Town. The hostel offers dormitories with shared bathrooms and living rooms. Black Swan also provides group activities and a kitchen.

Soul Backpackers

Diputación 323, 08009 L'Eixample, soulbackpackers.com

Looking to stay in Barcelona on a budget? This backpacker hostel might be just for you. They don't accept guests over 45 and offer mixed as well as women-only shared rooms. Chill in their hammocks or prepare yourself a tasty breakfast in the well-equipped kitchen.

St. Christopher Inn

Carrer de Bergara 3, 08001 L'Eixample, st-christophers.co.uk

Centrally located, cheap and full of good vibes. That's how we would describe this hostel that is only a two-minute walk from the famous Rambla and is also close to Plaça Catalunya. Enjoy a drink or your continental breakfast in the bar, or take a seat at their very Instagrammable Spanish patio. Guests receive discounts in some nearby bars and restaurants.

Sunotel Aston

Carrer de Paris 101, 08029 L'Eixample, sunotelaston.com

Looking for a little more luxury but don't want to break the bank? Sunotel might be the perfect place for you. The hotel has a rooftop swimming pool and offers comfortable rooms. It's a bit more on the upper side of L'Eixample and closely located to one of the biggest streets in Barcelona: Avinguda Diagonal.

Casa Gracia Hostel

Passeig de Gràcia 116, 08008 Gràcia, casagraciabcn.com

An attractive modern hostel located between Gràcia and L'Eixample, closely connected to the beautiful Passeig de Gràcia. You can book a private or shared room, or an apartment. On their shared terrace, Casa Gracia hosts events with live music and a happy hour. There's also a library room, as well as a kitchen.

Generator Barcelona

Carrer de Còrsega 377, 08037 Gràcia, staygenerator.com

Private or shared rooms close to the charming neighbourhood of Gràcia and well connected, with two metro stations close by. The colourful hostel has a rooftop bar with beautiful views over the city and offers various shared spaces with sofas and fun details like a pool table.

The Social Hub

Carrer de Cristóbal de Moura 49, 08019 Sant Martí, thesocialhub.co

In Poblenou, the most dynamic neighbourhood of the city, you will find this modern building, formerly known as The Student Hotel. The Social Hub includes a pool, co-working spaces, and a bar: everything at hand at one location. The perfect spot to connect with others and be inspired.

Inout Hostel

Carrer Major del Rectoret 2, 08017 Sarrià-Sant Gervasi, inouthostel.com

Camping vibes on the green hills of Collserola, this hostel with a private pool, surrounded by nature, is something else. All rooms face the beautiful Collserola park, just outside of the city. We love how this hostel focuses on sustainability and offers work opportunities to people with a labour market disadvantage.

model n.2

2
9
El Call

ENTRADA

GOOD TO KNOW

Language

Barcelona is a bilingual city: both Spanish (*castellano*) and Catalan are official languages. Catalan is widely spoken, and you'll see it used on most menus and public information signs. While Spanish will do the job in most situations, trying to use a few Catalan phrases will be greatly appreciated by locals. Common phrases include *Bon dia* (Good morning), *Si us plau* (Please), *Gràcies* (Thank you), and *Adéu* (Goodbye). But all locals will understand Spanish, and many in the tourism industry speak English.

Eating habits and mealtimes

Mealtimes in Barcelona differ from many other places. Breakfast, or *esmorzar*, is usually a light meal consisting of coffee and a pastry or a sandwich, often eaten around 9-11am. Lunch, or *dinar*, is the main meal of the day, typically eaten between 2 and 4pm. It usually includes multiple courses: a starter, main dish, dessert, and coffee. In the afternoon, around 5-6pm, people may have a small snack, such as a pastry or a sandwich, known as *merienda*. Dinner, or *sopar*, is generally lighter than lunch and eaten late, usually around 9-11pm, with people dining as late as midnight. Tapas are also a popular lunch or dining option. Many restaurants close between lunch and dinner, so plan accordingly.

Tipping

Tipping in Barcelona is not

obligatory but is appreciated for good service. It is customary to leave a small tip, about 5-10%, at restaurants. For smaller cafés or bars, rounding up the bill is sufficient. Tour guides, hotel staff and taxi drivers also appreciate tips, but generally they are not expected.

Nightlife and Clubbing

Barcelona has a vibrant nightlife that starts late and goes on until the early hours of the morning. Bars and pubs typically open around 6-8pm and get busy after 10pm, closing around 2-3am. Clubs often don't get going until 1-2am and stay open until 6am. Popular clubbing areas include the historic centre, L'Eixample, and the beachfront area of Port Olímpic and La Barceloneta. Many clubs have a dress code, usually smart casual, so avoid beachwear and overly casual attire. Some clubs charge an entry fee, which often includes a drink.

Shopping

Supermarkets in Barcelona open around 9am and stay open until 9 or even 10pm. Other shops usually open between 10 and 11am. Larger stores and shopping centres typically remain open throughout the day without a siesta break, while smaller shops in residential areas might close for a few hours in the afternoon, usually from 2 to 5pm. Outside of the major shopping areas, many shops close earlier, around 1pm, on Saturdays. Sundays are generally a day of rest, with most shops closed, except for those in major tourist areas and some corner shops.

Cultural etiquette

In Barcelona, a light kiss on each cheek (starting with the left) is a common greeting among friends and acquaintances, or even when meeting someone new. A handshake is standard in more formal settings. Dress

modestly when visiting religious sites and remember that swimwear is appropriate only at the beach or in pool areas. Officially, you are not allowed to walk around the city in swimwear. Spaniards tend to speak loudly, so noisy and bustling bars and restaurants are quite normal. However, try to keep noise levels down in residential areas, especially late at night.

Planning

If you're planning to visit iconic landmarks such as the Sagrada Família and Park Güell, it is highly recommended to buy your tickets online in advance. These attractions are extremely popular, and tickets sell out quickly, especially during peak seasons.
For the Sagrada Família, pre-purchasing tickets is not just about availability; you simply won't be able to buy tickets on the spot. Park Güell, known for its stunning mosaics and unique Gaudí architecture, also uses a time-slot ticket system to manage crowds. Most sights offer special prices for students and people under 30.

Safety

Like any major tourist destination, it's important to stay aware of your surroundings. Pickpocketing, unfortunately, is quite common, especially in crowded areas like La Rambla, El Gòtic, and on popular metro lines. Keep your valuables secure and out of sight, avoid carrying large sums of money, and consider using a money belt or an anti-theft bag. Be cautious of distractions, such as people asking for directions or offering help, as these can be tactics used by thieves.

Senyalització
Excepcional
Per obres

Maribel
Rebecca

WHEN TO TRAVEL

BARCELONA IN SPRING

Spring is probably our favourite season. April, May, and June are perfect for enjoying the lush greenery of Parc de la Ciutadella and Parc Güell. Cherry blossoms add a touch of magic to the city's landscape. Temperatures are perfect for strolling through the charming streets of El Gòtic and El Born, or a long lunch on a terrace.

For breathtaking views, head to Montjuïc Hill, Tibidabo, or Bunkers del Carmel. Enjoy the Mediterranean breeze as you cycle along the picturesque waterfront of La Barceloneta or enjoy a picnic on the golden sands of the city's beaches.

April brings not only green leaves and blooming flowers but also comes with lively festivities, including celebrations of Semana Santa, or Holy Week, and the Sant Jordi festival, Barcelona's Valentine's Day, when the streets are filled with roses and books to celebrate World Book Day.

As the sun warms the city, rooftop terraces and beach bars spring to life, offering the perfect setting to have a glass of sangria and soak up the vibrant atmosphere. Seek refuge from the urban bustle in Collserola Park, where you can enjoy panoramic views of the city.

Immerse yourself in the city's cultural scene during events like La Nit dels Museus, when museums open their doors late into the night, and enjoy the many outdoor festivals that are held in spring, such as Primavera Sound or the famous Brunch Electronik sessions.

BARCELONA IN SUMMER

In summer, Barcelona comes alive with warm temperatures, vibrant festivities, and, above all a relaxed Mediterranean vibe. There is no better time to enjoy the city's beaches, from the bustling La Barceloneta to the quieter shores of Bogatell and Mar Bella. Spend lazy afternoons at the beachfront *chiringuitos* (beach bars) or try your hand at water sports like paddle boarding. For panoramic views and cool breezes, head to Montjuïc Hill for the open-air cinema. In the evenings, enjoy the many beautiful squares in the Old Town.

June, July, and August also bring festivities to Barcelona, starting with the Sant Joan celebrations on 23rd June, when bonfires light up the evening sky and fireworks illuminate the beaches. Don't miss the popular Festa Major de Gràcia in August, when the streets of Gràcia are transformed into magical scenes with elaborate decorations and lively street parties. Another highlight is the iconic Sónar Festival, a celebration of electronic music and multimedia arts that attracts crowds from around the world.

Escape the heat exploring the city's cultural heritage with visits to iconic landmarks like the Sagrada Família and the Picasso Museum or look for shade in the city's leafy parks, such as Parc de la Ciutadella. At night, immerse yourself in the buzzing nightlife of Barcelona, with rooftop bars, beach clubs, and open-air concerts.

BARCELONA IN AUTUMN

Autumn arrives late in Barcelona. Usually, you can still enjoy warm weather well into October. You may still be able to swim in the sea when the first signs of autumn become visible at local markets, where you can find seasonal delights like chestnuts and an array of mushrooms.

Don't miss the opportunity to sample traditional autumnal treats like *panellets*, small almond-based pastries the locals enjoy during Día de Todos los Santos (All Saints' Day) on 1st November, a Barcelona bank holiday. Other worthwhile cultural events are La Mercè in September, the city's biggest festival with free concerts and activities all over town. At the end of October, La Castanyada is celebrated at schools, with a visit of a lady who brings chestnuts. The children's celebration includes special songs, activities, and hot chocolate. Autumn is full of opportunities to immerse yourself in the rich history and traditions of Barcelona. A tasty way of taking part is to buy roasted sweet potatoes or chestnuts from the little street kiosks that are only around at this time of year.

Autumn is perfect for exploring the city's parks and gardens. The changing foliage provides a colourful backdrop for a stroll and a picnic. For outdoor enthusiasts, autumn is also the time to explore the countryside and vineyards surrounding Barcelona, where you can enjoy scenic hikes, wine tastings, and harvest festivals. Take a day trip to nearby Montserrat or the Penedès wine region to experience Catalonia's autumn landscapes.

BARCELONA IN WINTER

As winter descends on Barcelona, the city takes on a festive charm with Christmas lighting everywhere. The city's iconic landmarks are all adorned in their seasonal decorations, from the illuminated façades of Casa Batlló to the Sagrada Família. There are various Christmas markets, along with events like Els Llums de Sant Pau, an annual light festival that turns the beautiful old modernist hospital 'Sant Pau' into a spectacular winter wonderland.

Both 25th and the 26th of December are bank holidays. The most important moment of the year for Catalan children is the arrival of the Three Kings on 6th January, with the impressive Cabalgata de Reyes parade.

It never gets very cold in Barcelona and the sunny winter days are perfect for long lunches on outdoor terraces or walks by the water side. Don't miss the opportunity to sample seasonal specialities like *turrones* (nougat) and *churros con chocolate*, perfect on a chilly winter afternoon. Locals love their winter dishes such as *escudella* or *carn d'olla* (a rich meat and vegetable stew). From January onwards, the traditional *calçots* (grilled spring onions) served with romesco sauce are definitely on every local's agenda.

Looking for outdoor fun? Winter in Barcelona offers the opportunity to explore the surrounding mountains and countryside, with activities like skiing and snowboarding just a few hours away.

de Nadal
St JOSEP
LA BOQUERIA

LIFE IN
RCELONA
SPAIN

HISTORY

Barcino: the origins

In the 1st century BCE, the Romans established a thriving settlement known as Barcino. With its strategic location on the Mediterranean coast, Barcino flourished as a centre of commerce. The Romans were responsible for the first parts of Barcelona's impressive architecture, such as the ancient city walls, the Temple of Augustus, and the aqueducts that supplied the city with water. The Roman legacy can still be felt in Barcelona, especially in El Gòtic and at the city's historical museum MUHBA, where remnants of Roman baths, mosaics, and other archaeological finds offer a glimpse into the city's ancient past.

Union with Aragón

In the 12th century, Barcelona joined the Crown of Aragón, a powerful maritime empire that dominated the western Mediterranean. This union brought economic prosperity and political stability, as Barcelona became a key player in Mediterranean trade routes. The Catalan language and culture flourished during this period, shaping Barcelona's identity. The city saw the construction of grand Gothic buildings. This era also marked the establishment of the Generalitat de Catalunya, the governing body in the region that has played a crucial role in maintaining Catalan autonomy and identity through the centuries.

14th & 15th Centuries

During the 14th and 15th centuries, Barcelona experienced a period of expansion and cultural flourish, marked by the construction of iconic landmarks, such as the Basilica of Santa Maria del Mar. It stands as a testament to the wealth and influence Barcelona gained through maritime trade. The period also saw the expansion of the city's defensive walls. Port de Barcelona was developed, growing into one of the most important ports of the Mediterranean. However, this time also saw the expulsion of Jews and Moors from Spain in 1492, which had a significant impact on the city's social fabric. Many citizens abandoned El Call, the Jewish quarter and intellectual centre of Catalonia, leading to a loss of cultural and economic diversity. Despite these challenges, Barcelona continued to thrive as a hub of commerce, art, and innovation, laying the groundwork for future growth.

18th Century

The 18th century brought tumultuous times to Barcelona, culminating in the War of the Spanish Succession in 1714. The city's support for the Habsburg pretender led to a devastating siege and loss of political autonomy. The aftermath of the war saw the suppression of Catalan institutions and the imposition of centrist policies by the Bourbon monarchy from Madrid. Despite these setbacks, Barcelona's spirit remained unbroken. The El Born Cultural and Memorial Centre, housed in a former market building, stands as a testament to Barcelona's determination to preserve its cultural heritage. This museum not only commemorates the events of 1714 but also serves as a cultural hub, showcasing the rich history and traditions of Catalonia.

Industrial Revolution

In the 19th century, Barcelona underwent rapid industrialisation, transforming from a medieval city into a modern metropolis. The textile industry emerged as a driving force of economic growth, attracting migrants from rural areas and other parts of Spain. The industrial expansion led to significant urban development, with the rise of new neighbourhoods like L'Eixample, designed to accommodate the growing population. Both factory halls and slums emerged across the city, especially in the Poblenou area, which became known as the 'Catalan Manchester' due to its dense concentration of factories. This era also saw the rise of labour movements and social reforms, as workers sought better conditions and rights, laying the foundation for Barcelona's modern social and political landscape.

World Exhibition & Catalan Modernism

The late 19th and early 20th centuries marked an age of creativity and innovation in Barcelona, illustrated by the Catalan Modernista movement. Iconic architects like Antoni Gaudí, Lluís Domènech i Montaner, and Josep Puig i Cadafalch left their marks on the city with masterpieces such as the Sagrada Família, Casa Batlló, and Palau de la Música Catalana. The 1888 and 1929 World Expositions showcased Barcelona's modernity and cultural richness to the world, solidifying its reputation as a global cultural capital. These events also spurred the development of infrastructure and public spaces, transforming Barcelona into a cosmopolitan city where tradition meets innovation.

Civil War

The Spanish Civil War (1936-1939) brought turmoil and tragedy to Barcelona. The city became a battleground between republican and nationalist forces. The bombing of civilian targets, such as the iconic Plaça de Catalunya, left scars that are still visible. Despite the devastation, Barcelona remained a symbol of resistance and solidarity. Its citizens worked closely together in support of the republican cause, organising community kitchens, hospitals, and defence committees. The war also fostered a spirit of artistic and intellectual defiance, with figureheads like George Orwell and Pablo Picasso making significant contributions to the republican effort.

Francisco Franco

During the Franco era (1939-1975), Spain was under authoritarian rule, marked by human rights abuses, political repression, censorship, and political persecution. Basic civil liberties were restricted, and political opponents were imprisoned or executed. Cultural and linguistic diversity was suppressed. Economically, Spain faced isolation and stagnation in the first decades of the Franco era. Despite these harsh conditions, underground movements and cultural resistance persisted in Barcelona, keeping the spirit of Catalan identity alive.

Democracy

From 1975, following the end of Franco's dictatorship, Spain transitioned to democracy, and a new era of political freedom and social change started. Barcelona played an important role in Spain's democratic transition, with its vibrant cultural scene and activist spirit. The city's first democratic elections in 1979 were a significant milestone,

Foot Locker

leading to the restoration of the Generalitat de Catalunya and the promotion of Catalan culture and language. Today, Barcelona stands as a beacon of democracy and diversity, with its citizens actively engaged in shaping the city's future. Festivals, public art, and a thriving civil society reflect the city's dynamic and inclusive spirit.

Summer Olympics

The 1992 Olympic Games marked a turning point in Barcelona's history, transforming the city into a global destination, revitalising its urban landscape. Iconic venues such as the Olympic Stadium and Port Olímpic were built, and Barcelona got its beach! The Games were also responsible for investments in public spaces and infrastructure, converting Barcelona into a modern prosperous city. The successful Olympics boosted the city's international profile and set the stage for its emergence as a major tourist destination, attracting millions of visitors each year.

Booming tourism

The Olympics laid the foundation for Barcelona's emergence as one of Europe's leading tourist cities. In recent decades, Barcelona has become one of the world's most popular destinations, attracting millions of visitors each year with its rich history, culture, and Mediterranean charm. However, dealing with this popularity is one of the biggest challenges of contemporary Barcelona. Ensuring that tourism remains sustainable, both for the natural environment and the local community, is a pressing issue. Efforts are being made to balance the benefits of tourism with the preservation of Barcelona's unique character and the quality of life for its residents.

SIGHTSEEING

Sagrada Família

Carrer de Mallorca 401, 08013 L'Eixample, sagradafamilia.org

Antoni Gaudí's masterpiece is probably Barcelona's most iconic landmark. Construction began in 1882 and continues to this day. The intricate façades and tower spires are adorned with detailed sculptures, each telling a different biblical story. Inside you will find Gaudí's concrete forest and the stained-glass windows creating a mesmerising play of light. Visiting the Sagrada Família is a must, but be sure to book your tickets in advance.

Casa Batlló

Passeig de Gràcia 43, 08007 L'Eixample, casabatllo.es

A UNESCO World Heritage Site, this is one of Gaudí's most famous residential buildings. Located on Passeig de Gràcia, its façade is a masterpiece of colourful mosaics and organic shapes. The building's interior is equally stunning, with its waving walls, beautiful woodwork, and stained-glass windows. A visit to Casa Batlló offers a deep dive into Gaudí's innovative architectural style and his ability to blend functionality with artistic expression.

Casa Milà

Passeig de Gràcia 92, 08008 L'Eixample, lapedrera.com

Also known as La Pedrera, Casa Milà is another of Gaudí's architectural marvels on Passeig de Gràcia. This Modernista building is renowned for its undulating stone façade and wrought-iron balconies that may remind you of waves and seaweed. Inside, Gaudí surprises with his innovative use of space and light. The rooftop, with its surreal chimneys and ventilation towers, offers panoramic views of Barcelona.

Casa Amatller

Passeig de Gràcia 41, 08007 L'Eixample, amatller.org

You'll find yet another majestic building on the same street as Casa Milà and Casa Battló. This former residential building is a stunning example of Modernista architecture by Josep Puig i Cadafalch, designed on behalf of chocolatier Antoni Amatller. With its intriguing façade, the *casa* blends Gothic and Flemish influences. Don't miss the chocolate shop on the ground floor, a nod to the Amatller family's confectionery legacy.

↓ SAGRADA FAMILÍA

↓ CASA MILÀ

Park Güell

Carrer d'Olot 5, 08024 Gràcia, parkguell.barcelona

Another one of Gaudí's creations, this colourful, fairy-tale-like park is located in Gràcia. Originally intended to be a residential area, it's now a public park filled with the typical *trencàdis* mosaics, winding paths, and playful structures. The park offers stunning views of the city and a chance to explore Gaudí's imaginative vision. Highlights include the serpentine mosaic bench and the famous lizard sculpture *El Drac*. Don't forget to book your entry for the monumental zone in advance, as it requires a ticket.

La Rambla

La Rambla, 08002 El Gòtic, El Raval

This is probably the most famous street in Spain, stretching from Plaça de Catalunya to the Columbus Monument at the old port, Port Vell. The bustling boulevard is lined with shops, cafés, and street performers, making it a lively spot for a stroll. The Mercat de Sant Josep de la Boquería, a vibrant market where you can try freshly prepared tapas and other local delicacies, is a must-visit. La Rambla is always buzzing with activity, but do keep an eye on your belongings as it's a well-known spot for pickpockets.

Arc de Triomf

Passeig de Lluís Companys, 08003 El Born

This arch was built as the entrance for the 1888 Barcelona World Fair and inspired by its Parisian counterpart. It is made of red brick and adorned with sculptures representing industry, commerce, and arts. The wide promenade between the popular Parc de la Ciutadella and the arch is a popular spot, perfect for a leisurely walk, people-watching, or enjoying street performances.

Torre Glòries

Avinguda Diagonal 211, 08018 Sant Martí, miradortorreglories.com

Formerly known as Torre Agbar, Torre Glòries is a modern skyscraper that has become a symbol of contemporary Barcelona. Designed by Jean Nouvel, its distinctive shape quickly earned it a variety of (naughty) nicknames from the locals. The tower houses offices and offers an observation deck with stunning views over the city. At night, the building's dynamic LED light displays don't go unnoticed in the cityscape.

↓ PARC DE LA CIUTADELLA

↓ ARC DE TRIOMF

Camp Nou

Carrer d'Aristides Maillol 12, 08028 Les Corts, fcbarcelona.com/tickets/camp-nou-experience

For football fans, a visit to Camp Nou is basically essential. This iconic stadium is home to FC Barcelona and has witnessed countless historic matches. The stadium tour takes you to the locker rooms, press rooms, and even the pitch. You can also visit the FC Barcelona Museum, which showcases the club's rich history, including trophies, memorabilia, and interactive displays. Whether you're a die-hard fan or just curious, Camp Nou offers an exciting glimpse into the world of Barcelona's beloved football club.

Barcelona Cathedral & El Gòtic

Pla de la Seu, 08002 El Gòtic, catedralbcn.org

The Gothic Quarter, or Barri El Gòtic, is a living open-air museum and one of Barcelona's most enchanting neighbourhoods, filled with narrow, winding streets and historical charm. At its heart stands the magnificent Barcelona Cathedral, an example of Gothic architecture and a must-visit landmark. El Gòtic is also home to El Call, the historic Jewish quarter, where you can learn about the rich cultural heritage of Barcelona's Jewish community. Wandering through the maze-like alleys, you'll find a mix of cosy cafés, artisan shops, and hidden squares, each with its own story.

↓ CASA AMATLLER

↓ CASA BATLLÓ

↓ PARK GÜELL

MUSEUMS

Museu Picasso

Carrer de Montcada 15-23, 08003 El Born, museupicassobcn.cat

At this museum, you can take a deep dive into the early works of Pablo Picasso, who lived in Barcelona as a youngster. Situated in El Born, it houses an extensive collection of thousands of pieces, providing a fascinating insight into Picasso's development and connection to Barcelona. It's a must-visit for anyone interested in art and history.

Moco Museum

Carrer de Montcada 25, 08003 El Born, mocomuseum.com/locations/barcelona

Contemporary and modern art brought to life in a fun and accessible way. Located in the El Born district, this museum showcases works by iconic artists like Banksy, Andy Warhol, and Salvador Dalí. It's especially popular among young people who want to experience cutting-edge, activist, and rebellious art. Don't miss the digital immersive art room by Studio Irma.

MACBA (Museu d'Art Contemporani de Barcelona)

Plaça dels Àngels 1, 08001 El Raval, macba.cat

Barcelona's contemporary art museum can be found in the Raval district. The museum's sleek, modern design by architect Richard Meier is quite a sight. Inside, you'll find a diverse collection of works from the mid-20th-century to the present, with a focus on Catalan and Spanish artists.

Museu Marítim

Avinguda de les Drassanes 1, 08001 El Raval, mmb.cat

The Maritime Museum of Barcelona, located in the historic Drassanes Reials (Royal Shipyards), offers a fascinating look at the city's seafaring past. The museum features impressive ship models, maritime artefacts, and objects related to the history of navigation in Barcelona. It gives insight to anyone interested in nautical history and the role of the sea in shaping Barcelona.

CCCB (Centre de Cultura Contemporània de Barcelona)

Carrer de Montalegre 5, 08001 El Raval, cccb.org

Located in the vibrant Raval district, the Centre de Cultura Contemporània de Barcelona (CCCB) is a hub for contemporary culture. The museum hosts a variety of exhibitions, film screenings, and cultural events that explore urban culture, digital innovation, and contemporary thought. With its dynamic and ever-changing programming, the CCCB is unmissable if you're interested in contemporary Barcelona culture.

↓ HEMP MUSEUM GALLERY

↓ MOCO MUSEUM

Museu de l'Art Prohibit

Carrer de la Diputació 250, 08007 L'Eixample, museuartprohibit.org

The 'Museum of Forbidden Art' is dedicated to showcasing works that have been censored or banned throughout history. Located in L'Eixample, the museum presents art that has challenged societal norms and has provoked thought worldwide. It's a unique place that encourages visitors to reflect on the power of art and freedom of expression.

Museu del Disseny de Barcelona

Plaza de las Gloria Catalanas 37-38, 08018 Poblenou, dissenyhub.barcelona

Are you a design lover? The Design Museum of Barcelona can be found in the modern 22@ district. It celebrates innovation in design, from everyday objects to avant-garde fashion. Exhibits cover various disciplines, including industrial design, graphic design, and decorative arts. Get inspired by the creativity and ingenuity of designers from around the world!

Hemp Museum Gallery

Carrer Ample 35, 08002 El Gòtic, hashmuseum.com

This museum in El Gòtic explores the history and uses of the cannabis plant. It covers everything from its medicinal properties to its role in popular culture. It's an eye-opening experience that sheds light on a plant that turns out to have played a significant role in human history for thousands of years.

Museu d'Història de Barcelona (MUHBA)

Plaça del Rei, 08002 El Gòtic, barcelona.cat/museuhistoria

Take a journey to Barcelona's rich past in the Historical Museum of Barcelona. Located on several historic sites across the city, the main location in El Gòtic allows you to walk through Roman ruins beneath the city streets and see the interior of one of the most important buildings from medieval times. The museum offers a comprehensive look at Barcelona's development from ancient times to the present day.

Fundació Joan Miró

Parc de Montjuïc, 08038 Sants-Montjuïc, fmirobcn.org

This museum, located on Montjuïc Hill, celebrates the works of Barcelona-born Joan Miró, a pioneering figure in surrealism. Its collection includes paintings, sculptures, and textiles that reflect Miró's imaginative and playful style. The building itself, designed by Miró's friend Josep Lluís Sert, is an architectural gem that offers beautiful views of the city.

MUSEU DE L'ART PROHOBIT

"Art allows us to bring up uncomfortable questions."

JOSEPHINE MECKSEPER

MNAC (Museu Nacional d'Art de Catalunya)

Parc de Montjuïc, 08038 Sants-Montjuïc, museunacional.cat

This museum is housed in the stunning Palau Nacional on Montjuïc Hill. It offers an extensive overview of Catalan art, from Romanesque church paintings to modernist masterpieces. The panoramic views of Barcelona from the museum's terrace are a bonus, especially when the sun sets.

CosmoCaixa

Carrer d'Isaac Newton 26, 08022 Sarrià-Sant Gervasi, cosmocaixa.org/cosmocaixa-barcelona

This is an interactive science museum for curious minds. It features a variety of hands-on exhibits, covering topics from space exploration to rainforest ecosystems. Its standout attraction is the Flooded Forest, a living Amazonian ecosystem. This museum makes learning about science fun for visitors of all ages.

Museu de Ciències Naturals

Plaça Leonardo da Vinci 4-5, 08019 Sant Martí, museuciencies.cat

The Museu de Ciències Naturals, located in the beautiful Parc del Fòrum, is a fantastic place to explore the wonders of nature. It features engaging exhibits on geology, palaeontology, and biodiversity, with a special focus on the natural history of Catalonia. It's a fun and educational destination for young and old.

STREET ART

When it comes to street art, the streets of Barcelona are a willing canvas. Local artists like to use the medium to raise awareness about relevant issues, turning it into something much more than just decoration. It is a very powerful form of expression too. In the 1970s, at the end of the Franco era, street art slowly began to emerge, and it really took off after the 1992 Olympics. But there was an ongoing discussion: is it art or vandalism? In 2006, the local government introduced hefty fines for painting in public places. This led many artists to leave. It hasn't stopped new pieces from emerging, although some of them are legal. There are a lot of galleries taking street art inside and to new levels, so you could even take a piece of it home.

Artevistas Gallery

Passatge del Crèdit 4, 08002 El Gòtic, artevistas.eu

Nestled in El Gòtic, this gallery is known for its dynamic collection of street art, mainly made by local artists. It focuses on emerging artists, giving you a glimpse into the future of urban art. The exhibitions are constantly changing, so there's always something new to see. The gallery is housed in the beautiful Passatge del Crèdit. Many more urban art pieces can be found in the surrounding area too.

Base Elements

Carrer d'Avinyó 31, 08002 El Gòtic, baseelements.net

This gallery is a hidden gem in the same neighbourhood. It also puts a strong emphasis on local artists, and you may even be able to see them creating their newest pieces as the owner offers artists a studio. Don't forget to take a peek in the basement, where some of their unfinished work and spray paints can be found.

Montana Gallery

Carrer Comerç 6, 08003 El Born, montanagallerybarcelona.com

This shop and gallery is a must-visit for street art enthusiasts. Located in El Born, this shop was Barcelona's first point of sale for the local graffiti spray paint brand Montana Colours (MTN) and other supplies, and it played an important role in the graffiti scene in the last few decades. The gallery showcases works by local and international street artists.

Àgora Juan Andrés

Carrer de l'Aurora 13, 08001 El Raval, agorajuanandres.wordpress.com

Welcome to the Àgora community garden in memory of Juan Andrés Benitez. Benitez was a well-known entrepreneur from Gayxample (the LGBTQ+ neighbourhood in L'Eixample), who in 2013 died at this spot due to police violence. Locals took possession of this vacant lot after the tragedy. The outside wall depicts the incident, while inside, you will find anti-capitalist murals.

Keith Haring

MACBA, 08001 El Raval, haring.com/!/art-work/241

One of the most iconic pieces of street art in Barcelona is Keith Haring's *Todos juntos podemos parar el SIDA* ('Together We Can Stop AIDS'). This mural, located in the Raval neighbourhood, was created in 1989 as a public awareness message during the AIDS crisis, reflecting Haring's social activism through art. Haring, who in 1990 died of complications from AIDS himself, chose El Raval specifically due to its high rates of AIDS, at the time often linked to drug use in the area.

Hangar

Carrer Emilia Coranty 16, 08018 Sant Martí, hangar.org

An artist residency and production centre located in Poblenou. While Hangar primarily focuses on contemporary art, it also supports street artists by providing them with space and resources to create. The surrounding area often features murals and graffiti created by resident artists.

Me Lata

Ciutat Vella

This Catalan artist duo from Barcelona have been creating street art since 2014. Their works consist of recycled cans painted with positive messages. They work in both Spanish and English. You can find their cans scattered throughout the old town. Their name, Me Lata, is a play on words involving the word 'can' (*lata*) and the Spanish verb for the beating of a heart (*latir*).

ÀGORA JUAN ANDRÉS

CINEMA

A trip to the cinema is always a great way to spend a rainy day. In Barcelona, most cinemas screen their films dubbed into either Spanish or Catalan. To find films in their original version, look for the following abbreviations: *VO* (*Versión Original*) indicates the original version without any subtitles, and *VOSE* (*Versión Original Subtitulada en Español*) means the original version with Spanish subtitles.

Filmoteca de Catalunya

Plaça de Salvador Sequí 1, 08001 El Raval, filmoteca.cat

Located in Raval, this film archive and screening centre showcases a wide range of films, from restored classics to avant-garde contemporary works. The Filmoteca is dedicated to preserving and promoting Catalan as well as international cinema.

Verdi Cinemas

Carrer de Verdi, 32, 08012 Gràcia, cines-verdi.com

Verdi Cinemas, located in vibrant Gràcia, is a favourite among film enthusiasts. Known for its eclectic mix of independent, international, and classic films, Verdi is an alternative to a mainstream cinema experience.

Renoir Floridablanca

Carrer de Floridablanca 135, 08011 Sant Antoni, cinesrenoir.com

Renoir Floridablanca is situated in the lively Sant Antoni area and offers a curated selection of quality films from around the world, in their original language. After watching the film, take a stroll through the trendy streets of Sant Antoni.

Sala Montjuïc

Fossat de Sant Eulàlia, 08038 Sants-Montjuïc, salamontjuic.org

Every summer, this open-air cinema sets up in the beautiful Montjuïc Castle gardens, offering a unique way to enjoy both classic and contemporary films. Bring a blanket and some snacks, and enjoy the warm evenings with friends as you watch films projected onto the backdrop of the castle walls.

FESTIVALS

Sant Jordi

Barcelona's romantic and literary festival is celebrated on 23rd April. The city fills with book stalls and flower vendors, as traditionally people give each other roses and books.

Primavera Sound

One of the coolest music festivals in Europe attracts music lovers from all over the world. Held in late spring at Parc del Fòrum, it features a diverse lineup ranging from indie rock and hip-hop to electronic and experimental music.
primaverasound.com

Sónar

The ultimate festival for electronic music and digital arts enthusiasts. This three-day event in June combines cutting-edge music with multimedia art, tech, and creativity.
sonar.es

Sant Joan

This local celebration of the summer solstice is held on the evening and night of 23rd June. Barcelona's beaches become the centre of the celebrations, with bonfires, fireworks, music, and dancing until dawn.

Festa Major de Gràcia

One of Barcelona's most beloved neighbourhood festivals takes place mid-August. The streets of Gràcia are transformed with elaborate decorations created by locals. There is live music, dancing, parades, and plenty of other activities.
festamajordegracia.cat

La Mercè

Barcelona's biggest annual festival, held in September to honour the city's patron saint La Virgen de la Mercè. The streets come alive with parades, fireworks, concerts, and traditional Catalan events like *castellers* (human towers) and *correfocs* (fire runs).

Brunch Electronik

A series of Sunday events that run from spring to autumn, perfect for those who love daytime partying. Held in different outdoor locations, it features top electronic and house DJs, street food, and a chill vibe.
barcelona.brunchelectronik.com

Palo Alto Market

This trendy, urban market happens on the first weekend of the month in a beautiful old factory in Poblenou. Featuring street food, live music, designer stalls, and art installations, it attracts a young crowd.
palomarketfest.com

TOURS

Street Art Tour

This tour is dedicated to the city's street art and graffiti scene. Explore the most important murals and hidden spots where graffiti thrives. Learn about the history, techniques, and local and international artists shaping the street art movement.

streetartbcn.com/street-art-barcelona-urban-tour

Treasure Hunt

Barcelona is the perfect backdrop for an exciting treasure hunt. The narrow, winding streets of El Gòtic form a labyrinth of clues and puzzles, each designed to lead you to hidden gems, squares, and famous landmarks. This challenge is a unique way to explore the city.

treasurehuntbarcelona.com

Free walking tour

Explore the heart of Barcelona with a free walking tour through the historic centre, which usually takes you through the vibrant old streets of El Gòtic. You'll hear fascinating stories about the rich history and culture. Don't forget to tip your guide.

freetour.com/barcelona
freewalkingtoursbarcelona.com

Tapas Tour

Foodies must take a tapas tour. Explore hidden gems and popular spots alike, where you'll savour classic bites like *patatas bravas* or *tortilla*. Along the way, you'll learn about the history and traditions behind these treats.

secretfoodtours.com/barcelona/food-tours-barcelona

Crimes Tour

Discover Barcelona's dark side with this thrilling walking tour through the old town, unravelling the city's most terrifying true crime. Wander through El Raval, El Gòtic, and El Born as your guide shares chilling details of historic crimes that shook Barcelona for decades. This tour will leave you with a different perspective on the city's streets and landmarks.

ohmyguidebarcelona.com/tour/crimes-the-tour

THINGS TO DO

Mercat de Sant Josep de la Boqueria

Barcelona's most famous market is a foodie's idea of heaven. Here you can find everything from fresh seafood and exotic fruits to local delicacies like *jamón ibérico* and Spanish cheeses. The perfect place to grab a fresh juice or a quick bite.

La Rambla 91, 08001 El Raval, boqueria.barcelona

Beach Life

There are several beaches in the city, such as La Barceloneta, Nova Icària, and Bogatell. The beach scene is lively and social, with plenty of beach bars, *chiringuitos*, offering refreshing drinks and snacks, and a wide variety of activities, such as surfing and paddleboarding.

Rent a Bicycle

Exploring Barcelona by bike is a fantastic way to see the city. You can ride along the beachfront or through the bustling streets of the city centre, discovering hidden gems at your own pace.

Paradox Museum

A mind-bending experience that's both fun and educational. With a series of interactive and illusion-based exhibits, it challenges your perceptions and plays with reality.

Plaça d'Urquinaona 3, 08010 L'Eixample, paradoxmuseumbarcelona.com

Bunkers del Carmel

These former anti-aircraft bunkers, located on Turó de la Rovira hill, offer a stunning 360-degree view of the city. It's a short hike to one of the best views.

Carrer de Marià Labèrnia, 08032 Horta-Guinardó, bunkers.cat

Tibidabo

This historic amusement park, located on the city's highest mountain, has been entertaining visitors for over a century. It offers a mix of thrills and breathtaking views. Climb to the top of the church, the Temple of the Sacred Heart.

Plaça del Tibidabo 3-4, 08035 Sarrià-Sant Gervasi, tibidabo.cat

↓ MERCAT DE SANT JOSEP DE LA BOQUERIA

Levi's

FAMOUS PEOPLE

Antoni Gaudí

One of the most renowned architects in history, Gaudí has left an indelible mark on Barcelona. His unique and innovative style is evident in numerous buildings throughout the city, most famously the Sagrada Família, which remains unfinished to this day. Gaudí's work is characterised by his use of organic shapes. Some of his other famous designs include Park Güell, Casa Batlló, and La Pedrera. Gaudí's impact reaches beyond architecture, deeply influencing the identity of Barcelona.

Rosalía

The flamenco sensation who has taken the global music scene by storm, was born in a small town just outside of Barcelona. Rosalía is known for her modern interpretation of traditional flamenco music. Her breakthrough album *El Mal Querer* earned critical acclaim and numerous awards. Rosalía's dynamic performances and innovative music videos have made her a cultural icon, bridging the gap between traditional Spanish music and global pop.

Johan Cruyff

Although originally from the Netherlands, Johan Cruyff became an adopted son of Barcelona through his profound impact on football club FC Barcelona. First as a player and later as coach, Cruyff revolutionised the club's playing style and philosophy. Under his leadership, Barça achieved numerous victories, including their first European Cup in 1992. Cruyff died in Barcelona in 2016.

Pablo Picasso

One of the most influential artists of the 20th century, Pablo Picasso spent his formative years in Barcelona. Although born in Málaga, Picasso moved to Barcelona as a teenager and immersed himself in the city's vibrant art scene. It was here that he developed his early style and began experimenting with the techniques that would lead to the creation of Cubism. Museu Picasso houses one of the most extensive collections of his works, offering a glimpse into his artistic evolution.

Lionel Messi

Often regarded as the greatest footballer of all time, Lionel Messi has a deep connection with Barcelona. Born in Argentina, he moved to Barcelona at a young age to join the FC Barcelona youth academy, La Masia. Over his career with the club, he shattered numerous records and led the team to countless victories, including multiple UEFA Champions League titles and La Liga championships. Messi's unparalleled skills, vision, and dedication to FC Barcelona made him a beloved figure in the city.

Montserrat Caballé

This legendary soprano was born in Barcelona and became one of the most celebrated voices in opera. Montserrat Caballé is perhaps best known for her collaboration with Freddie Mercury on the song *Barcelona*, which became the anthem for the 1992 Olympics held in the city. Her contribution to the arts and her enduring legacy are still celebrated in Barcelona's cultural institutions.

Pep Guardiola

This Barcelona native is a highly respected football

manager and former player. Pep Guardiola began his career at FC Barcelona, where he was a key part of the 'Dream Team' under Johan Cruyff. As coach, Guardiola led Barça to an unprecedented era of success, including winning 'the treble' in 2009 (the three major trophies in a single season: the domestic league La Liga, the domestic Copa del Rey, and the UEFA Champions League). His tactical genius and emphasis on possession-based football have influenced coaches worldwide, making him one of the most successful and admired figures in the sport.

Gerard Piqué

Born and raised in Barcelona, Gerard Piqué is a renowned footballer who has enjoyed a successful career with FC Barcelona. Known for his strong defensive skills and leadership on the field, Piqué has been instrumental in the team's numerous victories, including multiple Champions League and La Liga titles. Off the field, he is also known for his business ventures and his former relationship with pop star Shakira.

Marta Sierra

A rising star in the world of fashion and social media. As a Barcelona-based influencer, Marta Sierra has garnered a large following. Sierra's influence extends beyond fashion; she is also known for promoting local brands and showcasing the beauty of Barcelona through her photography. Her work has made her a prominent figure in the city's modern cultural landscape.

Manu Chao

This world-famous singer has deep ties to Barcelona. Although born in Paris to Spanish parents, Manu Chao's music often reflects his Spanish heritage and the multicultural influences of his upbringing. Known for his eclectic style, which blends rock, reggae, and Latin sounds, Manu Chao has been a prominent figure in the city's alternative music scene. His songs often address social and political issues, resonating with audiences worldwide. Bar El Mariatchi, in El Gòtic, is said to be his favourite bar in town, and you may even bump into him here.

George Orwell

Renowned British author George Orwell spent a significant period in Barcelona during the Spanish Civil War. His experiences in the city and his participation in the conflict profoundly influenced his writing. Orwell's book *Homage to Catalonia* provides a vivid account of his time in Barcelona and the political climate at the time.

Isabel Coixet

Film director Isabel Coixet is known for her thought-provoking films that often explore complex human emotions and relationships. Coixet has made a significant impact on contemporary cinema. Her works, such as *My Life Without Me* and *The Secret Life of Words*, have received international recognition.

Mercè Rodoreda

One of Catalonia's most important writers was born in Barcelona. Mercè Rodoreda's novels, including *The Time of the Doves*, are translated worldwide. Rodoreda's work often delves into themes of identity, memory, and the impact of war. She remains a literary icon in Barcelona.

Laia Sanz

Champion motorcyclist who won multiple world championships, Laia Sanz is a Barcelona native. Her determination, skill, and perseverance have earned her a prominent place in the traditionally male-dominated sport, inspiring many young athletes in Barcelona and beyond.

FILMS & SERIES IN AND ABOUT BARCELONA

Vicky Cristina Barcelona (2008)

This romantic comedy-drama by Woody Allen stars Scarlett Johansson, Rebecca Hall, Javier Bardem, and Penélope Cruz. It follows two American friends, Vicky and Cristina, who spend a transformative summer in Barcelona and get entangled in a complicated love affair with a charismatic artist and his fiery ex-wife. The movie not only delves into themes of love and self-discovery but also highlights Barcelona's architecture and vibrant streets. The city's beauty plays a key role in enhancing the film's romantic and dramatic atmosphere, making it a captivating watch.

Todo sobre mi madre (All About My Mother, 1999)

Directed by the famous Spanish filmmaker Pedro Almodóvar, this acclaimed drama tells the story of a nurse who moves to Barcelona after the tragic death of her son to find his father. The film explores themes of loss, identity, and human connection, all set against the backdrop of Barcelona's eclectic streets and landmarks. With its rich visual storytelling and powerful performances, this film is a must-watch for those who appreciate deep, character-driven dramas that resonate on multiple levels.

800 metros (800 Meters, 2022)

This gripping miniseries delves into the 2017 terrorist attacks in Barcelona and Cambrils. Through interviews and dramatizations, it provides a detailed account of the events and their impact on the city. An informative series that offers insight into a significant moment in Barcelona's recent history.

La catedral del mar (The Cathedral of the Sea, 2018)

Based on the bestselling novel with the same name, this historical drama series is set in 14th-century Barcelona and follows the life of a young serf who dreams of freedom. The series brings medieval Barcelona to life, showcasing the construction of the iconic Santa Maria del Mar in the neighbourhood of El Born. Highly recommended for those interested in Barcelona's history.

Bird Box Barcelona (2023)

A spinoff from hit film *Bird Box* (2018) which starred Sandra Bullock, this horror-thriller takes the terrifying concept to the streets of Barcelona. It follows a new group of survivors as they navigate a dystopian world in which looking at certain entities can be deadly. The film offers a new perspective on the original story, within the setting of Barcelona.

Smiley, una historia de amor (Smiley, 2022)

This Spanish romantic comedy series follows the love story between two men in Barcelona who meet after a mistaken voicemail. It's a heartwarming and humorous exploration of relationships, set against the beautiful and diverse decor of the city. The series captures the ups and downs of love in a way that's both relatable and entertaining, making it a feel-good watch for anyone.

Hache (2019)

Set in the 1960s, this crime drama series revolves around a woman who becomes deeply involved in the heroin trade in Barcelona. With its noir aesthetic and gripping plot, Hache provides a dark and thrilling look at a different side of the city. The series combines historical context with intense storytelling.

Bienvenidos a Edén (Welcome to Eden, 2022)

This Spanish thriller series follows a group of young adults who are invited to an exclusive party on a remote island, only to discover that they're part of a sinister plan. While not set entirely in Barcelona, the series features scenes in the city and captures the intrigue and allure of its nightlife.

Velvet Coleccíon (Velvet Collection, 2017-2019)

A continuation of the popular Spanish *Velvet* series, this drama follows the fashion house Velvet as it opens a new shop. The story centres around the fashion house as it expands its empire with a new boutique in the glamorous city of Barcelona. The series blends romance, drama, and high fashion, with the city's stylish and sophisticated side playing a central role.

Merlí (2015-2018) & Merlí: Sapere Aude (2019-2021)

This beloved Catalan series and its spin-off follow the life of a high school philosophy teacher and his students. Set in Barcelona, the series explores philosophical themes and teenage issues. Definitely an engaging and thought-provoking series that gives an insight into Barcelona's educational institutions and urban life.

Parfum (Perfume, 2018)

Loosely inspired by Patrick Süskind's classic novel *Perfume*, this German-Spanish series combines crime, mystery, and psychological thriller elements. Set in both Germany and Spain, it includes scenes in Barcelona. The story revolves around a series of murders linked to a group obsessed with creating the perfect scent.

Who is Erin Carter? (2023)

This action-packed thriller series centres around a British expat living in Barcelona. Her seemingly ordinary life spirals out of control after a violent incident unexpectedly exposes her dark and mysterious past. The series is filled with gripping twists and turns that will leave you guessing until the very end. It's highly recommended for anyone who enjoys fast-paced narratives that are rich with intrigue, danger, and unexpected surprises.

BOOKS IN & ABOUT BARCELONA

La sombra del viento (The shadow of the wind) – Carlos Ruiz Zafón

Set in the first half of 20th-century Barcelona, this captivating novel follows a young boy named Daniel who discovers a mysterious book in the Cemetery of Forgotten Books, situated in the old city centre. As he delves deeper into the story, he uncovers dark secrets about the book's author and his own family. This novel is the first in a four-part series, offering an immersive experience of Barcelona's streets and history.

La Catedral del Mar (Cathedral of the Sea) – Ildefonso Falcones

This historical novel transports readers to 14th-century Barcelona, where a serf named Arnau Estanyol arrives in Barcelona while the city builds the magnificent Santa Maria del Mar cathedral in El Born. Through Arnau's journey, readers experience the social and political turmoil of medieval Barcelona.

Barcelona Dreaming – Rupert Thomson

A captivating novel composed of three interconnected novellas, set on the eve of the global financial crash. Through the eyes of diverse narrators, including a middle-aged English woman, a jazz musician, and a literary translator, this novel vividly portrays both the charm and complexity of Barcelona. The stories delve into themes of love, immigration, and the city's vibrant culture. Thomson makes readers yearn for Barcelona's dreamy neighbourhoods, lively streets, and rich history.

134

La ciudad de los prodigios (The City of Marvels) – Eduardo Mendoza

Spanning from the 1888 World Fair to the 1929 Universal Exposition, this novel chronicles the life of Onofre Bouvila, an ambitious young man who climbs the social ladder in Barcelona. His story intertwines with the city's transformation into a modern metropolis.

Victus: Barcelona 1714 – Albert Sánchez Piñol

This historical novel takes you to the Siege of Barcelona during the War of the Spanish Succession, one of the most important moments in Catalan history. Through the eyes of Martí Zuviría, an engineer turned soldier, you'll witness the intense struggle and resilience of Barcelona's inhabitants. Highly recommended for history enthusiasts, and with detailed technical battle descriptions.

Barcelona – Robert Hughes

This non-fiction book by renowned art critic Robert Hughes offers an in-depth exploration of Barcelona's history, culture, and architecture. Hughes' narrative spans from the Roman era to the modern day, highlighting key events and figures that shaped the city. An essential read for anyone looking to understand Barcelona beyond its tourist attractions.

Homage to Catalonia – George Orwell

In this memoir, George Orwell recounts his experiences fighting in the Spanish Civil War on the side of the Republicans. Orwell's observations of the political dynamics and the harsh realities of war provide a unique perspective on Catalonia and Barcelona during a turbulent period.

The Struggle for Catalonia – Raphael Minder

Journalist Raphael Minder delves into the complex political and cultural identity of Catalonia in this comprehensive book. He examines the region's history, the rise of the independence movement, and its impact on Barcelona. Minder offers readers an understanding of the ongoing conflict and its significance for the city's future.

Homage to Barcelona – Colm Tóibín

Colm Tóibín guides readers from the city's founding and explosive 19th-century growth to modern times, bringing to life figures like Antoni Gaudí, Joan Miró, and Salvador Dalí. He delves into Catalan nationalism, the Spanish Civil War's tragedies, and the Franco dictatorship's impact, having witnessed the transition from dictatorship to democracy in the 1970s and 1980s. Tóibín also captures Barcelona's essence as a city of churches, museums, and creativity and innovation.

Barcelona Shadows – Marc Pastor

Set in the dark alleys of early 20th-century Barcelona, *Barcelona Shadows* is a chilling thriller based on the horrific and true crimes of Enriqueta Martí, the 'Vampire of Barcelona'. The novel follows Inspector Moisès Corvo as he delves into the underbelly of the city to hunt down the infamous child murderer, uncovering the terrifying secrets hidden in the shadows.

MERCAT
St JOSEP
LA BOQUERIA

FUN FACTS

Barça vs. Barna

First things first: locals call the city *Barna*, not *Barça*. Barça refers exclusively to the city's famous football club, FC Barcelona. So, if you want to sound like a local, remember this distinction!

The Never-ending story of Sagrada Família

One of Barcelona's most iconic landmarks, the Sagrada Família, has been under construction since 1882. Designed by Antoni Gaudí, this magnificent basilica is famously unfinished. The ongoing construction is expected to continue for several more years, making it a true never-ending story.

No beaches until '92

Believe it or not, Barcelona's beaches are a relatively recent addition. Before the 1992 Summer Olympics, the city's coastline was industrial and inaccessible. The beaches were created as part of a major urban regeneration project for the Olympics, transforming the city into a leading beach destination.

The dark past of the Old Town

The now bustling and popular historical centre of Barcelona, known as El Gòtic, used to be a no-go area. In the middle of the 20th century, it was run-down and considered dangerous. Extensive renovations and revitalisation projects have turned it into a must-visit area filled with charming medieval streets, lively cafés, and shops.

Ghost stations

Barcelona's metro system has twelve ghost stations, or *estaciones fantasmas*. These are abandoned or unused stations that can sometimes be glimpsed from inside the train while passing them. Some were closed due to low passenger numbers, while others were never fully completed.

Rambla or Ramblas?

When people talk about La Rambla, they refer to the famous street that stretches from Plaça de Catalunya to the Christopher Columbus Monument. But did you know Barcelona has five different Ramblas? They include La Rambla de Catalunya, La Rambla de Poblenou, and La Rambla del Raval, each offering its own unique vibe and attractions. The term *rambla* itself is synonymous with the type of street, featuring a pedestrian walkway in the middle. Interestingly, the famous La Rambla is composed of five connected sections, each with its own character and charm, and therefore is often called *Ramblas*.

Star Wars

Did you know that some of the chimneys on top of Gaudí's Casa Milà (La Pedrera) inspired the design of the Stormtroopers' helmets in Star Wars? These uniquely shaped chimneys have become iconic, blending Gaudí's creative genius with pop culture.

Catalan Valentine's Day

In Barcelona, Valentine's Day has a local twist. While 14th February is celebrated, the main romantic holiday is on 23rd April, known as La Diada de Sant Jordi, or Saint George's Day. On this day, couples exchange books and roses, turning the city into a vibrant marketplace filled with stalls selling them as tokens of love.

Capital of Spain

During the Spanish Civil War (1936–1939), Barcelona briefly served as Spain's capital, from October 1937 to January 1939. This decision was a result of the Republican government's control over Catalonia. Amidst political turmoil, Barcelona became a symbol of republican resistance. However, as the nationalist forces gained ground, the capital shifted to Girona briefly before settling in Madrid.

Statue of Liberty in Barcelona

Did you know that Barcelona has its own version of the Statue of Liberty? You can find it at the Arús Library, in L'Eixample. Sculptor Manuel Fuxà was commissioned to make a copy to scale for the inauguration of the library in 1895 and it has been there ever since.

PHOTO SPOTS

El Beso

Carrer dels Ases 10, 08003 El Gòtic

For a romantic photo, head to *El Beso*, a colourful mosaic mural in El Gòtic (see page 90). Officially called *El món neix en cada besada* ('The world begins with every kiss'), this mural features thousands of individual tiles, each containing a tiny photograph. Stand close for a detailed look, or step back to capture the full image of two lips locked in a kiss.

Pont del Bisbe

Carrer del Bisbe, 08002 El Gòtic

This Gothic-style bridge is one of the most photographed spots in El Gòtic. Pont del Bisbe, or the Bishop's Bridge, spans Carrer del Bisbe and is a beautiful example of neo-Gothic architecture. The intricate carvings combined with the narrow street below are perfect for Insta-worthy shots. Early morning, when hardly anyone is around, is the best time.

Palau de la Música Catalana

Carrer Palau de la Música 4-6, 08003 El Born, palaumusica.cat/es

This stunning concert hall is a UNESCO World Heritage Site. Its colourful stained glass, beautiful mosaics, and grand façade make it a photogenic marvel. If you can, take a guided tour to capture the details of the interior too.

Casa Batlló

Passeig de Gràcia 43, 08007 L'Eixample, casabatllo.es

Another Gaudí masterpiece that's perfect for photography. Its fairy-tale like, undulating façade and dragon-scale roof are visually stunning. Visit in the early morning to capture the best light and avoid the crowds. The interior is equally photogenic with its organic shapes and impressive stained-glass windows.

Plaça de Gaudí

Carrer de Lepant 278, 08013 L'Eixample

For an iconic view of the Sagrada Família, head to Plaça de Gaudí. This small park offers a fantastic perspective of Gaudí's masterpiece reflected in the small pond. Early morning or late afternoon provides the best light for stunning photos. The contrast of the greenery with the towering basilica creates a postcard-perfect shot. You may have to queue.

Casa Milà

Passeig de Gràcia 92, 08008 L'Eixample, lapedrera.com

Also known as La Pedrera, Gaudí's architectural masterpiece is a prime location for photography enthusiasts. Its rooftop is particularly enchanting, featuring a surreal landscape of whimsical chimneys and ventilation towers with panoramic views of Barcelona. Visit early in the morning or late in the afternoon to take advantage of the soft natural light and to avoid the crowds. The rest of the building, with its flowing lines and decorative elements, also provides plenty of photogenic opportunities.

Park Güell

Carrer d'Olot, 08024 Gràcia, parkguell. barcelona

One of Gaudí's most famous creations, Park Güell is a mosaic wonderland. The colourful tiles, organic shapes, and panoramic views of Barcelona make it a must-visit for photographers. The famous lizard sculpture at the entrance, known as *El Drac*, is a particularly popular photo spot.

Piscines Montjuïc

Avinguda Miramar 31, 08038 Sants-Montjuïc, picornell.cat

These outdoor pools, set against the backdrop of the city, were built for the 1992 Olympics. Whether you're swimming or simply taking in the amazing view, it's a great photo spot. The pool bar Salts is accessible without an entry ticket.

Tibidabo

Plaça del Tibidabo 3, 08035 Sarrià-Sant Gervasi, tibidabo.cat/en

Barcelona's highest hill is home to an amusement park as well as the beautiful Temple Expiatori del Sagrat Cor. The views from there are spectacular. The colourful ferris wheel, the church, and the panoramic cityscape make for unique photos.

Bunkers del Carmel

Carrer de Marià Labèrnia, 08032 Horta-Guidardó, bunkers.cat/es

For one of the best panoramic views of Barcelona, climb up to the Bunkers del Carmel. This former anti-aircraft defence spot offers a 360-degree view of the city. Bring a picnic and your camera for a memorable photo session. The bunkers close early in the evening.

L'Hivernacle

Parc de la Ciutadella, Passeig de Picasso 1, 08003 Ciutat Vella

Nestled within the lush surroundings of Ciutadella Park, this is a hidden gem. The beautiful greenhouse, constructed in 1884, features stunning iron and glass architecture that creates a captivating play of light and shadow. The interior is filled with a variety of exotic plants.

FOOD AND DRINKS

BREAKFAST & BRUNCH

Art i Sa

A cosy brunch spot in the heart of the city. With locations in El Gòtic and Sant Martí, this charming café offers a delightful selection of breakfast and brunch options, from freshly baked pastries to hearty sandwiches, all made with locally sourced ingredients.

artisa.es

Brunch & Cake

Known for their beautiful food presentation and decor. You can find Brunch & Cake at different locations throughout the city, and they all have the same menu filled with great brunch dishes such as avocado toast, bowls, and smoothies. Their cakes and pastries are delicious too.

brunchandcake.com

Eixampeling

Pastel colours, floral walls, and a delicious menu: this is your place to go for an all-day Instagrammable brunch. They serve healthy as well as not-so-healthy brunch options, as well as cocktails and bubble tea. Something for everyone!

Carrer de la Diputació 158, 08015 L'Eixample, eixampeling.com

Bloom

Two locations that serve a very good brunch all day. Their location at Passeig de Sant Joan has positive affirmations written on the walls and their interior would fit any Instagram feed superbly. Did we mention that everything is gluten-free?

insta @bloombcn

Billy Brunch

Five different locations spread throughout the city centre. At each branch, you will find their tasty menu filled with brunch classics like eggs benedict, pancakes, and açai bowls. Accompany this with a festive mimosa or opt for a healthy smoothie.

billybrunch.com

Coco House

Fancy a fruity bowl or a smoothie on your way to the beach? Stop at Coco House! It's owned by the same people as Bloom who named this place after their dog Coco. Like the name suggests, you can get different coconut dishes here. But there are other options as well, such as specialty coffee, acai-bowls and pastries.

Carrer de Meer 52, 08003 La Barceloneta, cocohouse.es/coco

Trópico

You will find tropical vibes in the middle of the city. It's like going on a trip through Latin America and Asia without leaving Barcelona. On their menu you will find *arepas* and tacos but also smoothie bowls, fresh juices, and much more.

Carrer de Balmes 24, 08007 L'Eixample, insta @tropicobcn

Morning Glory

Run by Juanma and his mother, this cosy and authentic brunch spot will steal your heart. Delicious food in a homely atmosphere. Everything is home-made with local ingredients and most importantly, made with love. On their walls, you will find art from local artists.

Carrer de la Riereta 15, 08001 El Raval, morninggloryben.net

Lulu & Flynn

Hang on this terrace while sipping on a locally roasted specialty coffee or a freshly made smoothie. Here you will find real food. Not a morning person? At night you can go for drinks or order a glass of natural wine with a Mediterranean tapa. Very dog friendly too.

luluandflyn.com

Lato

The perfect spot for brunch or a quick coffee break. Their minimalist modern interiors create a relaxing atmosphere, and their menu features a variety of brunch favourites, freshly baked goods, and specialty coffee. Whether you're in L'Eixample or Ciutat Vella, Lato offers a delightful retreat from buzzing Barcelona.

en.latocafe.com

Alsur

With two locations in the city centre, Alsur is a vibrant café that brings together a diverse menu and an inviting atmosphere. From hearty brunch dishes to creative cocktails, it's a great place to start your day or unwind in the evening. Don't miss their delicious pastries and specialty coffee.

alsurcafe.com

COFFEE

Syra Coffee

Fancy a specialty coffee paired with some delicious pastry? Look for your nearest Syra Coffee. There are seventeen different branches spread out over Barcelona. All beans come from organic and fair-trade suppliers, and they will always put the quality of the coffee first.

syra.coffee

Nomad

What started as a barista stand on food markets in London, converted into a local success in Barcelona: Nomad coffee. Visit their coffee lab in the very Instagrammable and historical Passatge Sert. You will be surprised by the number of bean varieties.

Passatge Sert 12, 08003 El Born, nomadcoffee.es

Good news

Do you like to read a newspaper while you sip on your iced latte? Pop by a Good News newsstand. These typical newspaper kiosks serve good coffee and offer a collection of interesting books & magazines. You'll find them at different locations.

goodnewsco.es

La Roseta

Hidden in the old fisherman neighbourhood of Barcelona, you will find La Roseta. Their pastries and sweet treats are absolutely delicious, and they offer coffee roasted by Nomad. Win-win! Perfect for a little break close to the beach.

Carrer de Meer 37, 08003 La Barceloneta, insta @larosetabarceloneta

LUNCH & DINNER

La Central Burgers

One of the better burger places in town. You will find them centrally located between El Born and El Gòtic. All burgers are charcoal grilled, and veggie options are available.

Via Laietana 45, 08003 El Gòtic, centralburgers.es

Bo de B

Known for serving one of the absolute best (and biggest) sandwiches in Barcelona. Be prepared to queue and bring cash as it's not possible to pay by card. Worth it though. Fetch a sandwich before heading to the beach and enjoy your lunch after a dip in the sea.

Carrer de la Mercè 35, 08002 El Gòtic

Bar Oviso

Want to experience Barcelona like a local? Head to this bar on Plaça George Orwell. In the middle of El Gòtic, you will find this triangular space filled with sunny terraces. Enjoy a beer and have some food amongst the locals.

Carrer de n'Arai 5, 08002 El Gòtic

↓ EL NACIONAL

↓ XURROS IN CARRER DE PETRITXOL

fresh and flavourful dishes like pho, banh mi, and spring rolls in a lively setting that captures the essence of Vietnamese street dining.

Carrer del Comerç 17, 08003 El Born, lavietnamita.com

Fast Eddie's

Fast food at its best. Here you can try what some call the best burgers in town. Their menu is small, usually offering only two or three types of burgers available until they sell out. Make sure to arrive early!

Carrer dels Carders 6, 08003 El Born

Mosquito

A popular spot for Asian tapas and craft beers. Located in El Born, this cosy eatery offers a variety of dim sum, dumplings, and other Asian delights, making it a perfect place to enjoy a casual meal with friends. Their impressive beer selection is a bonus.

Carrer dels Carders 46, 08003 El Born, mosquito-bcn.com

La Vietnamita

Vietnamese street food paired with cocktails, perfect for those late summer nights that turn into pre-drinks. Enjoy

Tucco

Tucco offers a unique dining experience with homemade pasta and Argentinean-inspired dishes. This charming eatery in El Born provides a lively atmosphere and delicious yet very affordable meals that make it a favourite among locals and tourists alike.

Carrer del Consolat de Mar 23, 08003 El Born, tucco.com

Rosa Negra

Mexican food, margaritas and *micheladas* anyone? At Rosa Negra, you'll find yourself in Mexico without breaking the bank. Very affordable tasty food paired with great cocktails. Start your evening here, and you will have a great time for sure.

Carrer dels Àngels 6, 08001 El Raval, rosanegrarestaurantes.com

Time Out Market Barcelona

This vibrant food hall gathers some of the best chefs, local eateries, and gastronomic delights under one roof. Located in the scenic waterfront area, this lively market allows visitors to indulge in a variety of dishes ranging from traditional Catalan tapas to international cuisine, all handpicked by the editors of Time Out. The market offers an exciting blend of flavours, whether you're in the mood for fresh seafood, gourmet burgers, or delectable pastries.

Moll d'Espanya 5, 08039 El Gotic, timeoutmarket.com/barcelona

Parking Pizza

A must-visit for pizza lovers visiting Barcelona. Housed in a former parking garage, this trendy eatery combines industrial chic decor with a laid-back atmosphere. Known for its delicious wood-fired pizzas, Parking Pizza uses fresh, high-quality ingredients. The open kitchen allows guests to watch the skilled chefs at work, adding to the lunch or dining experience.

Passeig de Sant Joan 56, 08009 L'Eixample, parkingpizza.com

Gelida

Go to Gelida for an authentic Catalan dining experience. This spot is known for its traditional tapas and hearty mains. The rustic setting and friendly service provide a genuine local feel, making it a great place to enjoy a casual meal.

Carrer de la Diputació 133, 08011 L'Eixample, gelidabcn.com

Lalola

Experience traditional Spanish cuisine with a modern twist

AMSTEL
VERMUTS · VINS · PLATETS
VERMUT

MORITZ

in the former bullring Arenas de Barcelona. This stylish restaurant offers a range of tapas, paellas, and other classic dishes, all made with fresh, local ingredients. The welcoming atmosphere and excellent service make it a great choice for any meal.

Gran Via de les Corts Catalanes 373-385, 08015 L'Eixample, lalolabcn.com

Snack 55

For a quick and satisfying bite. This casual eatery offers a variety of sandwiches, salads, and snacks, making it a great stop for a light lunch or an afternoon nibble. The friendly service and central location make it a convenient choice.

Passeig de Sant Joan 55, 08009 L'Eixample, snack55.com

Carabela

Nestled in the heart of Barcelona, Carabela offers a fusion of Mediterranean and Latin American cuisine. With its relaxed atmosphere, it's an excellent spot for a laid-back lunch or dinner. Enjoy their delicious cocktails and dishes like tacos, burritos and fajitas. We also love their large terrace.

Pas de Sota Muralla 3, 08003 La Barceloneta, carabelabcn.com

Surf House

Cool place, right next to the beach, that also rents out SUP boards. Good for any time of the day, as they serve brunch, lunch, and dinner. With its relaxed beachside vibe, Surf House offers a perfect spot to unwind with friends and enjoy a tasty meal or a refreshing drink.

Carrer d'Emília Llorca Martín 22, 08003 La Barceloneta, surfhousebarcelona.com

Dr. Zhang

Step into one of Dr. Zhang's locations for a taste of Asia in the heart of Barcelona. This eatery offers an array of delicious dumplings and Asian-inspired dishes that are perfect for sharing. Their flavourful menu and friendly atmosphere make it a must-try for lunch or dinner.

drzhangbcn.com

Ugarit

Syria's flavours in Barcelona. Known for their delicious kebabs and mezze, Ugarit offers a warm and inviting atmosphere perfect for a relaxed meal with friends or family. Their generous portions and authentic flavours will probably make you want to come back to one of their restaurants.

ugarit.es

Honest Greens

Honest Greens is all about fresh, wholesome food that's both nutritious and delicious. This trendy spot focuses on seasonal, locally sourced ingredients to create salads, hearty bowls, and mouth-watering plates that cater to all dietary preferences. With its modern decor and commitment to healthy eating, Honest Greens has become one of the most popular spots in town for both vegans and vegetarians. They have various restaurants around town.

honestgreens.com

TAPAS

Jai-ca

A beloved spot in La Barceloneta, known for its delicious tapas and informal atmosphere. Specialising in seafood, you'll find fresh prawns, calamari, and other delights from the sea. Preferably enjoyed with a cold beer or a glass of vermouth. Perfect for a true taste of Barcelona's culinary tradition.

Carrer de Ginebra 13, 08003 La Barceloneta, jaica.com

Can Paixano (La Xampanyeria)

Step into Can Paixano for a

lively and authentic Catalan experience. Known for its cava and tapas, this bustling spot offers a taste of Barcelona's bar culture. Enjoy a glass (or bottle) of their own sparkling cava paired with a variety of delicious tapas and sandwiches.

Carrer de la Reina Cristina 7, 08003 La Barceloneta, canpaixano.com

Casa Lolea

Famed for its artisanal sangria, this is a cute restaurant with a very Spanish decor that complements their menu of traditional Spanish tapas and creative dishes. Ideal for a relaxed meal with friends, sharing some of their signature sangria blends.

Carrer de Sant Pere Més Alt 49, 08003 El Born, casalolea.com

Bormuth

Tucked in the lively El Born neighbourhood, go to Bormuth for a fantastic selection of traditional tapas with a modern twist. Their menu features dishes like patatas bravas, croquettes, and Iberian ham, all perfect for sharing. Pair your meal with a glass of vermouth for the true local experience.

Carrer del Rec 31, 08003 El Born, bormuth.com

Bar del Pla

For a genuine tapas experience, head to Bar del Pla in El Born. This cosy bar serves a variety of mouthwatering dishes, from succulent meats to fresh seafood. While it is a bit more expensive than some other options, the friendly atmosphere and excellent service make it one of our favourites.

Carrer de Montcada 2, 08003 El Born, bardelpla.com

Carrer Blai

This vibrant street in the Poble-sec neighbourhood is

famous for its many pintxo bars. Each one offers a variety of these delicious small bites on skewers, allowing you to hop from bar to bar. A fun, affordable, and must-do experience for any food lover.

Carrer de Blai, 08004 Sants-Montjuïc

Els Tres Tombs

Located between the vibrant El Raval district and foodie haven Sant Antoni, this is a classic bar with a rich history. With an extensive beer selection and hearty Catalan dishes, it's the perfect place to enjoy a relaxed meal or drinks with friends. The outdoor terrace is ideal for people-watching.

Ronda de Sant Antoni 11, 08011 L'Eixample

Bar Lobo

Right off La Rambla you will find Bar Lobo, a lively spot known for its delicious tapas and excellent service. You can see the street artists from the terrace, which is perfect to watch the world go by. The relaxed yet lively atmosphere makes it a place that's difficult not to like.

Carrer del Pintor Fortuny 3, 08001 El Raval, barlobo.com

La Monroe

Situated within the Filmoteca de Catalunya, this is a trendy spot perfect for brunch, lunch, or dinner. The eclectic menu ranges from Mediterranean cuisine to international favourites. With its stylish interior and vibrant terrace, it's a great place to enjoy good food and drinks in a cultural setting.

Plaça de Salvador Seguí 1, 08001 El Raval, lamonroe.com

Bar Calders

A favourite among locals. Bar Calders in the Sant Antoni area is a charming bar where you'll find many patrons standing outside, sipping a glass of wine while sharing

LOLEA

some tapas. The inviting atmosphere extends to the weekends, when the bar opens for lunch, offering a delightful spot to share some fusion dishes.

Carrer del Parlament 25, 08015 Sant Antoni, barcalders.com

XURROS

La Pallaresa Xocolateria Xurreria

Located in El Gòtic, La Pallaresa is famous for its thick, creamy hot chocolate and crispy churros. This traditional *xocolateria* has been serving locals and tourists alike since 1947. Don't be surprised if you see people queueing during the colder months of the year.

Carrer de Petritxol 11, 08002 El Gòtic

Granja M. Viader

Granja M. Viader is not just any café – it's the birthplace of the famous Cacaolat. This historic establishment offers a wide range of dairy delights, including fresh churros, pastries, and of course, the original Cacaolat. A must-visit for a taste of history.

Carrer d'en Xuclà 4-6, 08001 El Gòtic, granjaviader.cat

Granja Dulcinea

Step into Granja Dulcinea for a charming and an authentic experience. Known for its delicious hot chocolate and churros, this café has been a favourite since 1941. Perfect for an afternoon treat in the heart of El Gòtic. Located on the same street as La Pallaresa.

Carrer de Petritxol 2, 08002 El Gòtic, granjadulcinea.com

Xurreria Laietana

A classic spot for churros in Barcelona, one you could easily miss if you're not paying attention. Xurreria Laietana offers freshly made churros and *porras* (a lighter, less crispy variant of the traditional churro), perfect for dipping in rich hot chocolate.

Via Laietana 46, 08003 El Born

La Nena

A beloved spot in Gràcia, known for its homey atmosphere and sweet treats. Enjoy a cup of thick hot chocolate with freshly made churros, or explore their variety of cakes and pastries. Don't forget to grab one of the many board games from the cupboard. Ideal for families and friends.

Carrer de Ramón y Cajal 36, 08012 Gràcia, lanenagracia.com

BRING THE PARENTS

Cecconi's Barcelona

Cecconi's Barcelona, located in the Soho Club building, offers a taste of modern Italian sophistication in vibrant El Gòtic. This elegant restaurant is known for its classic Italian dishes and stylish ambience. The menu features handmade pasta and wood-fired pizzas, as well as fresh seafood and indulgent desserts. Highlights include the truffle risotto, lobster spaghetti, and creamy burrata.

Passeig de Colom 20, 08002 El Gòtic, cecconisbarcelona.com

4Gats

Immerse yourself in history and art at 4Gats, a legendary café-restaurant that was once a favourite of Picasso and other artists. Located in a Modernista building, it offers traditional Catalan cuisine with a touch of nostalgia. A perfect spot to share a cultural and culinary experience with your parents.

Carrer de Montsió 3, 08002 El Born, 4gats.com

El Nacional

Go to El Nacional for a unique dining experience. This beautifully restored former parking garage hosts multiple restaurants and bars under one roof, offering a variety of Spanish and

Mediterranean dishes. The elegant setting and different menu options make it perfect for a special family meal.

Passeig de Gràcia 24 Bis, 08007 L'Eixample, elnacionalbcn.com

Gallito

Located by the beach, Gallito offers a relaxed atmosphere with stunning views of the sea. Enjoy fresh Mediterranean-inspired dishes with a modern twist. Sit outside on the lovely terrace or reserve one of the stylish tables inside. We absolutely love their homemade paella.

Passeig del Mare Nostrum 19-21, 08039 La Barceloneta, gallito.es

BAR
CALDERS
BAR
ALARMA CONECTADA
SPITZ
93 451 75 00
BAR CALDERS
CERVESES
Estrella Galicia
TAP 1:
PILSNER URQUELL
TAP 2:
TAP 3:
Espiga

Cerveses

GOING OUT

BARS

Monk Barcelona

Tucked away behind what looks like a supermarket entrance, Bar Monk is a hidden gem in Barcelona's nightlife scene. Inside this speakeasy, you'll find an intimate setting with a cool, laid-back vibe. Their expertly crafted cocktails are a highlight, making Bar Monk a top spot to have a unique experience. Not cheap though, with prices starting at €15 for a cocktail.

Carrer dels Abaixadors 10, 08003 El Born, monkbarcelona.com

Bar Sauvage

This is where to go for a wild night out. This lively bar is known for its tropical cocktails and vibrant atmosphere. The jungle-themed decor and energetic vibe make it a fun place to start your night before heading to one of Barcelona's many clubs.

Passeig del Born 13, 08003 El Born, insta @barsauvagebcn

Mariposa

A chic cocktail bar known for its stylish interior. The intimate setting makes it a great spot for a date as well. Enjoy beautifully presented cocktails and note their wonderful-looking cocktail cups. These are made in the adjacent ceramics workshop.

Plaça de les Olles 4, 08003 El Born, mariposanegrabar.com

Nevermind

Nevermind attracts Barcelona's alternative scene. Located in both El Gòtic and El Raval, this bar combines a graffiti-covered atmosphere with a soundtrack of grunge, punk, and garage. The Carrer de Tallers venue even features a skate ramp for patrons to show off their tricks or just enjoy the spectacle. Nevermind is perfect for experiencing Barcelona's underground nightlife.

nevermindbcn.es

33/45

This is a trendy, laid-back bar perfect for a relaxed evening with friends. We like its eclectic decor, comfy seating, and great music. Don't forget to take a good look around as this bar is an art gallery as well.

Carrer de Joaquín Costa 4, 08001 El Raval, 3345.es

Bar Marsella

Bar Marsella, established in the 19th century, is a historic gem in El Raval offering a glimpse into Barcelona's past. The interior has remained virtually unchanged. Although famous for its absinthe, they also serve cocktails. Perfect for those seeking a classic Barcelona experience.

Carrer de Sant Pau 65, 08001, El Raval, insta @barmarsella

Dow Jones

At Dow Jones, stock market meets nightlife. You can order a wide range of beers, cocktails, and spirits with prices fluctuating based on demand, adding a fun and unique twist to your night out. Don't forget to check the screens before ordering. They have two bars; both can be found in L'Eixample.

dowjonesbar.com

George Payne

This is the go-to Irish pub in town. This bustling bar offers a welcoming atmosphere, with live music, sports on big screens, and an enormous selection of beers and whiskeys. It's the perfect spot for a lively night out and for meeting new people. Especially popular among the student crowd.

Plaça d'Urquinaona 5, 08010 L'Eixample, thegeorgepayne.com

Skyfall Cocktail Club

For breathtaking views and exquisite cocktails, head to Skyfall Cocktail Club. This rooftop bar offers a 360-degree view of the city. Dinner shows and other experiences are also on the menu.

Avinguda de la Granvia de l'Hospitalet 144, 08907 L'Hospitalet de Llobregat, skyfallbcn.com

Espit Chupitos

This budget-friendly bar is renowned for its extensive selection of *chupitos* (shots). With over 600 different shots to choose from, each priced at around €2, this popular spot guarantees a fun experience. Popular among students and young locals, Espit Chupitos has several locations across the city. Each shot comes with its own special twist.

espitchupitos.com

Ovella Negra

Ovella Negra, or 'Black sheep', is a popular tavern known for its lively atmosphere and large communal tables. It's the perfect place for groups to gather and enjoy jugs of sangria, pitchers of beer, and some cheap but tasty tapas. It's popular among both international and local students.

ovejanegra.es

CLUBS

Jamboree

Located in the heart of El Gòtic, at Plaça Reial, Jamboree is a renowned jazz club and nightclub after dark. It's known for its diverse musical lineup and intimate setting, and it's one of our favourites.

Plaça Reial 17, 08002 El Gòtic, jamboreejazz.com

Moog

For a high-energy night out in Barcelona, Moog is a popular choice. Located in El Raval, this small but iconic dance club has been a staple of the city's nightlife since 1998. The club is known for its fantastic sound system and diverse electronic music, including techno and house. There's a small room on the top floor too.

Carrer de l'Arc del Teatre 3, 08002 El Raval, moogbarcelona.com

Opium

Opium is one of Barcelona's premier beach clubs, offering a glamorous nightlife experience. With its beachfront location, stylish decor, and world-class DJs, Opium is a place to see and be seen.

Passeig Marítim de la Barceloneta 34, 08003 La Barceloneta, opiumbarcelona.com

Shoko

Shoko combines a restaurant and nightclub, making it a perfect spot for an all-in-one night out, right next to the beach. Start with a trendy meal in this Asian inspired club and end up dancing to top DJs and live performances, mainly of house music.

Passeig Marítim de la Barceloneta 36, 08003 La Barceloneta, shoko.biz

Pacha

Pacha Barcelona brings the iconic Ibiza brand to the city, offering a top-tier clubbing experience. With its famous twin cherries logo, Pacha attracts an international crowd and top DJs. Enjoy a night of dancing to the best house and electronic music in a legendary venue.

Carrer de Ramon Trias Fargas 2, 08005 La Barceloneta, pachabarcelona.es

Downtown

Downtown Barcelona is a hotspot for partygoers looking for a night of dancing and fun. It's one of the biggest dance clubs in town, with multiple dance floors and a variety of genres, including pop. Unlike the big clubs at the beach, Downtown is also very popular among locals.

Avinguda Dr. Marañon 17, 08028 Les Corts, downtownbarcelona.es

Razzmatazz

One of Barcelona's most iconic clubs, known for its huge dance floors and eclectic music

offerings. With five different rooms, each featuring different genres, Razzmatazz offers something for everyone: from indie rock to electronic beats.

Carrer dels Almogàvers 122, 08018 Sant Martí, salarazzmatazz.com

Apolo

Apolo is a legendary club housed in a stunning disused theatre. On weekends, it becomes the go-to spot for Barcelona's hipsters. Besides its vibrant club nights, Apolo also serves as a venue for dance and music performances, making it a cultural hotspot as well as a nightlife staple.

Sala Apolo, Carrer Nou de la Rambla 113, 08004 Sants-Montjuïc, sala-apolo.com

La Terrazza

For a unique open-air clubbing experience, head to La Terrazza. Located in the historic Poble Espanyol on Montjuïc Hill, this outdoor club offers some stunning views and a great atmosphere. Dance under the stars to the best electronic music in an enchanting setting.

Avinguda de Francesc Ferrer i Guàrdia, 08038 Sants-Montjuïc, laterrrazza.com

Bling Bling

For a touch of glamour, head to Bling Bling. This upscale club is known for its chic interior, VIP areas, and exclusive crowd. Expect a night of dancing to the best in house and electronic music and a sophisticated atmosphere.

Carrer de Tuset 8-10, 08006 Sarrià-Sant Gervasi, blingblingbcn.com

Mirablau Club & Disco

For a glamorous night out, Mirablau is the place to be. Situated halfway up Tibidabo Hill, this chic club offers stunning city views, stylish decor, and a sophisticated atmosphere. Enjoy expertly crafted cocktails, delicious tapas, and a mix of live DJ sets and smooth music while taking in the Barcelona skyline.

Plaça del Doctor Andreu s/n, 08035 Sarrià-Sant Gervasi, mirablaubcn.cat

SHOPPING

HOW TO DRESS LIKE A LOCAL

Barcelona is a city of both relaxed beach vibes and chic urban style. To blend in with the locals, you'll want to embrace a look that's both effortlessly stylish and comfortable. The warm Mediterranean climate calls for light, airy fabrics and loose-fitting clothes. Think linen shirts, flowy dresses, and wide-leg trousers. Pair these with comfortable yet stylish sandals, and you're ready to go.

Colours, floral prints, stripes, and polka dots add a fun element to your wardrobe, making your outfits as lively as the city itself. The city's bohemian neighbourhoods, such as Gràcia and El Raval, influence the local fashion with a touch of boho-chic. Think patterned scarves, statement jewellery, and unique, handcrafted accessories.

With Barcelona's stunning beaches just a stone's throw away, being beach-ready is a must. Stylish swimsuits, chic cover-ups, and wide-brimmed hats are everyday essentials. Sunglasses are not just for sun protection but a key accessory to complete your look.

The city's love for outdoor activities means that a casual, sporty vibe is also prominent. Athletic wear like leggings, sports tops, and sleek trainers are common sights, especially around parks and at beachfronts. Brands like Nike and Adidas are popular, seamlessly blending into the city's vibrant, active culture.

When night falls, Barcelona's nightlife scene comes alive, and the dress code shifts to smart casual. Think crisp shirts for men and stylish dresses or trendy tops paired with high-rise jeans for women. Comfortable yet stylish shoes are a must, as hopping between bars and clubs involves plenty of walking.

FLEA MARKETS, VINTAGE & SECOND-HAND

Barcelona is absolutely packed with vintage and second-hand shops as well as flea markets. On weekends, there's always a second-hand market somewhere, and you will find lots of charming boutiques in the old part of town, especially in El Raval and El Born. The growing emphasis on cutting down waste and being more environmentally aware in general sees new shops and markets opening all the time: rethink, reduce, reuse, and recycle. And why not have some fun along the way? You never know what you might find, but your new treasure could well be waiting for you at one of these locations.

Els Encants

Carrer dels Castillejos 158, 08013 L'Eixample, encantsbarcelona.com

One of Barcelona's oldest and largest flea markets, Els Encants is a paradise for vintage lovers. Here, you can browse through an eclectic mix of clothes, accessories, antiques, and more. Open Mondays, Wednesdays, Fridays, and Saturdays from 9am to 8pm, it's a must-visit for any second-hand enthusiast or collector. Also note the spectacular mirrored roof, a popular backdrop for selfies.

TurQuesh

Carrer de Sepúlveda 100, 08015 L'Eixample, turquesh.com

TurQuesh is a small but well-stocked vintage shop in Sant Antoni. It offers a variety of retro clothes, shoes, accessories, and other objects, all at reasonable prices. You may also encounter an exposition here.

Carrer Riera Baixa

Carrer Riera Baixa, 08001 El Raval

This street in El Raval is lined with vintage stores. There's a variety of shops, offering everything from retro fashion to unique accessories. Each has its own distinct vibe and collection. On Saturdays, a small vintage street market is set up here.

Lullaby Vintage

Carrer Riera Baixa 22, 08001 El Raval, insta @ lullaby_vintage_boutique

Lullaby Vintage is one of the shops located at Riera Baixa. It's a classic for pre-loved apparel and accessories. Everything is thoughtfully sorted by decade, making it easy to find unique earrings, bags, belts, hats, and clothes that reflect your personal style. Lullaby Vintage also features some musical memorabilia. Whether you're a vintage fashion enthusiast or a music lover, this is the perfect place to discover authentic and one-of-a-kind pieces in Barcelona.

Holala Plaza

Carrer de Valldonzella 2, 08001 El Raval, holalaibiza.com

Located in the heart of the city, Holala Plaza is more than just a vintage shop. It's a cultural space that combines fashion, art, and music. The shop offers a carefully curated selection of vintage clothes and accessories from around the world. For anyone looking for high-quality vintage pieces.

Flamingos Vintage Kilos

Carrer de Ferlandina 20, 08001 El Raval, flamingosvintagekilo.com

Familiar with the kilo shop concept? Flamingos Vintage Kilos offers vintage clothes priced by weight on two different locations in El Raval. With a vast selection of items from different eras, it's an exciting place to dig for treasure. The stock is continuously updated.

La Principal Retro & Co

laprincipalretro.com

A shop that specialises in clothes from the 70s, 80s, and 90s, sourced from across Europe. La Principal Retro & Co also features collections from young, up-and-coming designers and they have their own brand, барселона 92. There are two shops, both located in the vibrant Raval district.

Lost & Found

Plaça del Mar, 08003 La Barceloneta, lostfoundmarket.com/barcelona

A bi-monthly market that brings together the best of Barcelona's vintage and second-hand scene. Lost & Found is held at various locations: next to the beach as well as in the spectacular main hall of train station Estació de França. Usually there's more to be found than just clothes and accessories. Think: vinyl records and retro toys. Great atmosphere too.

Urban Vintage

Carrer dels Tallers 52, 08001 El Raval, insta @urbanvintage.barcelona

Handpicked selection of vintage urban streetwear, such as hoodies and T-shirts. Located in the neighbourhood of El Raval.

Le Swing

Carrer dels Lledó 6, 08002 El Born, leswingvintage.com

High-end vintage fashion in the trendy El Born district. With a focus on designer pieces from the 60s, 70s, and 80s, Le Swing is the perfect shop for glamorous, one-of-a-kind finds.

LOVE Vintage

Carrer de Bertrellans 5, 08002 El Born, lovevintage.es

Known for its carefully curated selection of vintage clothes, LOVE Vintage features items from the 70s, 80s, and 90s with a focus on bold, stylish pieces. A great spot for unique finds.

Humana

humana-spain.org

With multiple locations across the city, Humana is a popular chain of second-hand shops that support social and environmental causes. Here, you'll find affordable, preloved clothes and accessories. The location next to the Santa Caterina market in El Born specialises in vintage.

Moirai Market

Plaça dels Traginers 7, 08002 El Gòtic, moiraimarket.com

A concept store curated for vintage lovers, gem hunters, and sustainability supporters. Located in the heart of the city, this charming boutique offers an eclectic mix of one-of-a-kind finds and unique designs. From carefully selected vintage clothes and accessories to distinctive home deco and rare collectibles, Moirai Market is the perfect place for conscious shoppers.

Los Féliz

Carrer de Cervantes 5, 08002 El Gòtic, losfelizshop.com

Not a budget option: this boutique offers a carefully curated selection of mostly women's vintage designer pieces. Whether you're looking for a unique addition to your wardrobe or simply want to browse their collection, Los Feliz is a must-visit for vintage fashion enthusiasts.

Two Market

Carrer d'Àvila 78, 08005 Sant Martí, twomarket.es

The place to be for bargain hunters, Two Market hosts events where everything costs €1 per piece. Check their website for event dates and locations.

Revolution Vintage

Carrer de Verdi 80, 08012 Gràcia, revolutionvintagebcn.com

A treasure trove of second-hand goods in Carrer Verdi in Gracia. Specialising in urban vintage fashion, Revolution Vintage offers everything from dresses to shoes, jewellery to bags, lots of street style, and contemporary vintage. Unlike some second-hand shops that can be quite expensive, at Revolution Vintage you can find a real bargain.

Flea Market

fleamarketbcn.com

This famous Barcelona flea market brings buyers and sellers together at different locations. Flea Market organises events throughout town, at least once a month. Check their website for upcoming *mercadillos*.

Mahalo Vintage

mahalovintage.com

A shop for vintage fashion with a laid-back, beachy vibe. Here you'll find special designs, prints and unique cuts. Their shops can be found on two locations in the old city centre.

Kilo Store

Carrer de la Portaferrissa 25, 08002 Barcelona

Kilo Store is another vintage gem where clothes are sold by weight. This popular shop features a vast collection of retro fashion, from the 70s, 80s, and 90s, including everything from denim jackets and floral dresses to quirky accessories.

WARP

STREETWEAR

Kaotiko

Rambla de Catalunya 54, 08007 L'Eixample, kaotikobcn.com

This is probably Barcelona's most famous streetwear brand. It blends urban style with a touch of the city's unique flair, captured in bold colours and unique patterns. Go there for graphic tees, hoodies and accessories that complete any streetwear look. The somewhat rebellious pieces that are always creative are popular with local youngsters.

Solebox

Carrer del Pintor Fortuny 23, 08001 El Raval, solebox.com

A mecca for those looking for trainers. This high-end shop offers a curated selection of premium footwear and apparel from brands like Asics, New Balance, and their own exclusive collaborations. The shop's minimalist design is inspired by supermarket layouts.

Amigos Skate Shop

Carrer del Doctor Dou 16, 08001 El Raval, amigoskateshop.com

Amigos Skate Shop is a cornerstone of Barcelona's skate culture. Situated near MACBA square in El Raval, known as the city's best skate spot, this shop is a haven for skaters of all levels. They offer a vast selection of decks, trucks, wheels, and apparel from leading brands like Vans, Thrasher, and Santa Cruz.

Footdistrict

Carrer de la Lleona 4, 08002 El Gòtic, footdistrict.com

The ultimate place for trainer fans. Tucked away in the medieval heart of the city, this sneaker boutique offers a wide range of footwear from the likes of Nike, Adidas, and Puma as well as exclusive releases and limited editions. The interior is sleek and modern, contrasting with some beautiful historic details of the building.

DEPARTMENT STORES

El Corte Inglés

Plaça de Catalunya, 14, 08002 L'Eixample, elcorteingles.es

Spain's classic department store can be found at Plaça Catalunya. Everything from high-end fashion brands to electronics, homeware, and gourmet food is on offer. From the top floor you can enjoy stunning panoramic views of the city while grabbing a bite at the food court.

Arenas de Barcelona

Gran Via de les Corts Catalanes, 08015 L'Eixample, arenasdebarcelona.com

This unique shopping centre is housed in a former bullring on Plaça d'Espanya. The historic architecture has been preserved, with modern elements added. Inside, you'll find a mix of high-street and designer shops, as well as cafés, a gym and exhibition spaces. The rooftop terrace, with a variety of restaurants, offers stunning views of Montjuïc and the Magic Fountain.

Westfield Glòries

Avinguda Diagonal 208, 08018 Sant Martí, westfield.com/spain/glories

This modern shopping centre is situated in the trendy Poblenou district. It features an array of international and local brands, offering everything from fashion and beauty to technology and homeware. It also houses several restaurants.

Galerias Maldà

Carrer de la Portaferrissa, 22, 08002 El Gòtic

This hidden shopping centre is affectionately known as 'el Camden friki', inspired by London's famous Camden Market. It celebrates geek culture with a range of shops dedicated to popular franchises like Harry Potter, Dragon Ball, Pokémon, Lovecraft's universe, and Game of Thrones. You'll also find a speed cube shop, a puzzle store, and a board game shop in the Galerias.

↓ ARENAS DE BARCELONA

BOOKSHOPS

Altaïr

Gran Via de les Corts Catalanes 616, 08007 L'Eixample, altair.es

This is the perfect bookshop for travel enthusiasts. Located in L'Eixample, it specialises in travel literature, guides, and maps. If you're not planning your next adventure yet, Altaïr's extensive collection will definitely make you want to. The bookshop's staff can help you find the perfect book for your travels, and they also organise travel-themed talks and presentations.

Biblioteca García Márquez

Carrer del Treball 219, 08020 Sant Martí, ajuntament.barcelona.cat/biblioteques/es/bibgarciamarquez

Named after the famous Colombian writer Gabriel García Márquez, this library is located in the Sant Martí district. It offers an extensive collection of books in multiple languages, but it stands out for its architecture. This prize-winning library is well worth a visit. It offers modern design, cosy sitting areas, co-working facilities, and much more.

Come In Bookshop

Carrer de Balmes 129 Bis, 08008 L'Eixample, libreriainglesa.com

This shop might just have the largest selection of English books in the entire city. Step inside and marvel at the various book sections. Bonus: the staff are incredibly friendly and helpful. Nearby, at Provença 256, you'll find their department of language learning with a selection of textbooks, syllabi, dictionaries, and much more. Not only in English, but also in many other languages.

La Central

Carrer d'Elisabets 6, 08001 El Raval, lacentral.com

This is a favourite among local book lovers. Located in an old monastery in El Raval, this bookshop offers a wide range in various languages, with a strong focus on humanities and social sciences. The charming interior with wooden shelves is divided into different sections. Take your new book out to their terrace – it is one of the prettiest in the city.

Laie

Carrer de Pau Claris, 85, 08010 L'Eixample, laie.es

A beloved bookshop located near Passeig de Gràcia, Laie is known for its carefully curated selection of books across various genres, including fiction, non-fiction, art, and children's books. The shop also houses a café where you can enjoy a coffee and a snack while reading your latest purchase. Laie regularly hosts literary events and exhibitions.

Llibreria Quera

Carrer de Petritxol 2, 08002 El Gòtic, espaiquera.com

Llibreria Quera is a hidden gem for outdoor and adventure enthusiasts. Specialising in hiking, mountaineering, and climbing literature, this bookshop is located in El Gòtic. It offers guidebooks, maps, and manuals. You can book a table at the adjacent restaurant for some fantastic tapas.

The Hibernian

Carrer de Verdi 66, 08012 Gràcia, hibernianbooks.com

The Hibernian is an English-language bookshop located in the Gràcia neighbourhood. It offers a wide selection of new and second-hand books, from classic literature to contemporary fiction and non-fiction.

Mercat de Sant Antoni Sunday Market

Carrer del Comte d'Urgell 1, 08011 L'Eixample, mercatdesantantoni.com

Every Sunday, the area around the Mercat de Sant Antoni transforms into a bustling book market. Here, you can find a vast array of second-hand books, comics, magazines, and postcards. The market is a paradise for collectors and anyone looking for rare and out-of-print editions. It's also a great place to soak up the local atmosphere and enjoy a leisurely Sunday morning browsing through the stalls.

Ona

Carrer de Pau Claris, 94, 08010 L'Eixample, onallibres.cat

This is a unique bookshop dedicated to Catalan literature and culture. Situated in L'Eixample, it's the go-to place for anyone looking to dive into Catalan books, from classic literature to contemporary works. Even non-Catalan speakers will find this bookshop interesting because of its beautiful and playful modern design.

Re-Read

re-read.com

Re-Read is a chain of second-hand bookshops with several locations across Barcelona. This shop offers an eco-friendly and affordable way to enjoy reading, with a vast selection of pre-owned books at unbeatable prices. Their 'buy and sell' model encourages recycling and gives books a second life. Whether you're looking for a classic novel or a recent bestseller, Re-Read is the place to go for budget-friendly finds.

cafè restaurant
llibreriacafè
laie
RB
Vine al cafè
restaurant Laie

ART SUPPLIES

Raïma

Carrer Comtal 27, 08002 El Gòtic, raima.cat

One of the largest and most popular art supply shops in Barcelona. It has five floors with everything from high-quality papers, paints, and brushes to beautiful stationery and craft supplies. Whether you're a professional artist or a hobbyist, Raïma is a must-visit. Plus, the historic building, with a small bar and terrace on the top floor, is very appealing.

Belles Arts Ferran

Carrer de Ferran 39, 08002 El Gòtic, bellesartsferran.com

An art supply shop in bustling El Gòtic. It offers a wide range of art materials, from traditional to contemporary. You'll find high-quality paints, brushes, papers, and tools for all kinds of artistic endeavours.

Abacus

Carrer d'Ausiàs Marc 16, 08010 L'Eixample, abacus.coop

This huge store offers a wide range of art supplies, books, and educational materials. It's a great spot for artists and anyone into crafts. Their selection includes paints, sketchbooks, packaging materials, and much more. They can be found at multiple locations across the city.

Barna Art

Carrer de Còrsega 394, 08037 L'Eixample, barna-art.com

A go-to for artists looking for professional supplies. This shop specialises in fine art materials, including oil paints, acrylics, canvases, and easels. If you're looking for something specific, the staff will be able to advise you.

Pepa Paper

pepapaper.com

If you love beautiful stationery and design paper goods, or if you're into journaling, Pepa Paper is a must-visit. This charming shop offers an impressive selection of high-quality papers, notebooks, planners, and greeting cards, as well as craft supplies. They have various shops around town.

↓ RAÏMA

AFFORDABLE ART & HOME DECO

Chandal

Carrer d'en Tantarantana 16, 08003 El Born, chandal.tv

A cool independent shop that blends art, fashion, and home deco. You'll find a selection of retro-inspired prints, funky ceramics, vintage-style accessories, creative gifts, and stationery. Perfect for those who love to mix vintage charm and contemporary style.

↓ DESIGNPLACE

Fantastik

Carrer de Joaquín Costa 62, 08001 El Raval, fantastik.es

Fantastik is a treasure trove of quirky and eclectic items. The shop specialises in folk art and everyday objects from around the world. You'll find an array of colourful, unique items, from traditional Mexican masks to playful Japanese toys. It's also the perfect place to find a gift.

Galería Maxò

galeriamaxo.co

With different shops around El Born and El Gòtic, Galería Maxò offers an original selection of affordable art. The gallery is famous for its fun Barcelona photo frames, the perfect souvenir. You'll also find other works from local artists, including paintings and prints. Most are reasonably priced.

DesignPlace

lanostraciutat.co

This modern shop focuses on design souvenirs, such as prints, smaller art objects or coffee cups with a fun twist. With their own label as well as work from other Barcelona-based creatives, this is an amazing place for a fun, design-focused gift to bring home.

MoryArty

moryarty.com

At MoryArty, the walls are lined with design and beauty from another era. It is the perfect place for vintage prints and frames at very reasonable prices.

Vespa

RECORD SHOPS

Wah Wah Records

Carrer de la Riera Baixa 14, 08001 El Raval, wahwahrecords.bandcamp.com

If you're on the hunt for rare vinyl and eclectic sounds, this is a must-visit. Specialising in rare and obscure records, Wah Wah offers everything from 60s psychedelia to contemporary indie. A treasure trove for collectors.

Discos Paradiso

Carrer de Ferlandina 39, 08001 El Raval, discosparadiso.com

A vibrant, independent record shop in El Raval. Known for its extensive selection of electronic music, it is a favourite of DJs and dance music lovers. You can also find jazz, soul, funk, and hip-hop records, both new and second-hand. Regular in-store events, such as DJ sets and album launches, make Discos Paradiso a lively hub for the local music community.

Daily Records

Carrer de les Sitges 9, 08001 El Raval, dailyrecords.cat

Heaven for punk, ska, reggae, and Northern Soul enthusiasts. Founded in 1994 by Roger Geli, pioneer of Spain's skinhead culture, the shop has become a spiritual home for punk and similar movements. Their meticulously organised catalogue includes everything from 60s garage to heavy metal, attracting vinyl enthusiasts from around the world. Daily Records also has its own label.

Bite It! Records

Carrer de Ciudad Real 35, 08012 Gràcia, biteit-records.com

A dream for collectors of original USA and UK black music. With a passion for vinyl from the 50s, 60s, and 70s, Bite It! offers R&B, soul, funk, jazz, reggae, and Latin records. Please note that this shop is only open by appointment.

SHOPS WE LOVE

Ganiveteria Roca

Plaça del Pi 3, 08002 El Gòtic, ganiveteriaroca.com

This historic gem is known for its exceptional quality and extensive range of knives and cutlery. Established in 1911, this shop has been a staple for both professional chefs and home cooks. Check out the beautiful wooden interior and the Modernista entrance and displays.

Etnia Barcelona Flagship Store

Carrer de l'Espaseria 1-3, 08003, El Born etniabarcelona.com/es/en/stores/barcelona

This flagship store embodies the Barcelona-based eyewear brand's Mediterranean spirit and commitment to culture. Find yourself some fetching (sun)glasses, or explore their selection of art and culture books in a stylish wooden interior with lush greenery. Their stunning rooftop terrace offers views of Santa Maria del Mar.

Caganer Shop

caganer.com

A quirky chain where you can find a souvenir that captures the playful spirit of Catalan culture. They sell an astonishing variety of *caganers* – small figurines depicted in a defecating pose. Historically, these are placed in nativity scenes as a symbol of fertilisation and good fortune. The tradition extends to figurines of famous personalities, from celebrities and politicians to athletes and fictional characters.

I Wear Dolls

iweardolls.com

Get a unique bracelet, or design a beautiful necklace for a friend. At I Wear Dolls you will not only find ready-to-wear jewellery at very affordable prices, but you can also create your own. Handmade, waterproof, and unique. They also sell permanent pieces of jewellery that cannot be removed.

↓ ETNIA BARCELONA FLAGSHIP STORE

GREEN
BARCELONA

PARKS AND SWIMMING

The beach

The beach is one of the best things about Barcelona. There are several beaches within the city limits. Barceloneta Beach is undoubtedly the most popular, known for its lively atmosphere and proximity to the historic centre. For a more relaxed scene, head to Bogatell Beach, where you'll find locals playing volleyball and chilling out. Marbella is known as Barcelona's LGBTQ+ friendly beach. The coast is also perfect for water sports enthusiasts, offering activities like paddleboarding and kayaking.

Parc de la Ciutadella

Parc de la Ciutadella is Barcelona's most famous park. Nestled in the city centre, it's the perfect spot for a lazy afternoon. You can hire a boat and paddle around the lake, admire the Cascada Monumental fountain, or simply relax on the lawns. The park also houses Barcelona Zoo, Catalan Parliament, and various museums. It's a great place to hang out with friends, have a picnic, or join one of the many outdoor activities like yoga, dance or music sessions.

Parc de la Ciutadella, 08003 El Born

CNAB
(Club Natació Atlètic-Barceloneta)

For a more athletic swimming experience, head to Club Natació Atlètic-Barceloneta. Right on the beach, this sports club offers a range of swimming pools, including three outdoor pools with sea views. CNAB is perfect for those who want to swim some laps. The club also houses a gym, sauna, and other fitness facilities, making it a great place to keep fit and enjoy the beautiful beachfront location.

Plaça del Mar, 08003 La Barceloneta, cnab.cat

Collserola

For a nature escape within the city, head to the Collserola Natural Park. This vast green area is a haven for hikers, mountain bikers, and anyone looking to enjoy some fresh air and stunning views over Barcelona. The park is home to Tibidabo Mountain, where you can visit the iconic Tibidabo Amusement Park and Sagrat Cor church. The numerous trails and paths make it a great spot for outdoor adventures and an escape from the bustling city centre.

parcnaturalcollserola.cat

Cactus Garden & other parks on Montjuïc

Montjuïc is a treasure trove of parks and gardens, offering some of the best views of the city. The Cactus Garden, or Jardins de Mossèn Costa i Llobera, is a unique spot featuring a vast collection of cacti and succulents from all over the world. Wander the terraces and enjoy the panoramic vistas of the port and the Mediterranean. Montjuïc is also home to various other gardens, such as the Jardins de Joan Brossa, the Jardins de Laribal, and the charming Jardins del Teatre Grec, perfect for a leisurely stroll or a quiet picnic. Barcelona's Botanical Garden is located on the city hill as well, but unlike the other gardens, there is a small entrance fee.

Carretera de Miramar 38, 08038 Sants-Montjuïc

Swimming pool on Montjuïc

The Montjuïc Municipal Pool is a must-visit for a refreshing dip with a view. This outdoor pool, originally built for the 1992 Summer Olympics, offers stunning views over Barcelona. It's a popular spot for both locals and tourists looking to cool off in the summer heat. Take a dive and experience the Olympic vibe!

Avinguda Miramar 31, 08038 Sants-Montjuïc, picornell.cat

Parc del Laberint d'Horta

Escape the hustle and bustle of the city at Parc del Laberint d'Horta, one of Barcelona's best-kept secrets. This historic garden, located in the Horta-Guinardó district, features a charming neoclassical labyrinth made of cypress hedges. Get lost in the maze and explore the romantic gardens. It's a peaceful and picturesque spot, perfect for a quiet afternoon.

Passeig dels Castanyers 1, 08035 Horta-Guinardó

↓ PARC DE LA CIUTADELLA

VEGETARIAN AND VEGAN BARCELONA

When you think of Spanish cuisine, vegetarian and vegan options might not be the first thing that comes to mind. However, in Barcelona, you can find a wide range of delicious meat-free and plant-based meals. Most traditional restaurants have vegetarian options, and the number of vegan and vegetarian restaurants is growing. Even so, not all coffee places offer alternative milks yet. From quick bites to gourmet meals, here are some of the best vegetarian and vegan spots in the city.

Barna Brew Born

As the name suggests, Barna Brew is a must-visit for beer enthusiasts, offering an excellent selection of craft brews from around the world. This award-winning bar features ten rotating taps and a range of bottled beers. The experience is complemented by creative vegetarian burgers, like the Mexican Chickpea Burger, and healthier options such as parsnip fries. Vegan options are available.

Carrer de les Basses de Sant Pere 10, 08003 El Born

Blu Bar

This bar in the Poblenou area near the beach offers a variety of smoothies, fresh juices, and light, healthy dishes. The relaxed vibe and the great terrace make it an ideal spot to hang out with friends, sip on a smoothie, and soak up the atmosphere.

Rambla del Poblenou 11, 08005 Sant Martí, blubar.es

Faire Brunch & Drinks

Go to Faire for a fantastic vegetarian brunch experience. They serve specialty coffee and delicious locally sourced, organic, freshly prepared dishes. Faire also supports the mission to plant trees and promote environmental responsibility.

Carrer de Girona 81, 08009 L'Eixample, fairebrunch.com

Fat Veggies

Fat Veggies offers a unique and innovative take on plant-based cuisine dedicating itself to elevating vegetables to the star of each plate with a creative, complex, and delicious approach. Fat Veggies provides high-end vegetarian cuisine at affordable prices, making it a must-visit. This restaurant is especially famous for its grilled vegetables.

Carrer de Bailèn, 08009 Barcelona, L'Eixample, fatveggies.com

Flax & Kale

This is a health food haven that offers delicious flexitarian dishes. With a menu that's about 80% plant-based and 20% fish, this spot caters to all tastes while promoting a healthy, balanced diet. Their beautifully designed space and innovative dishes make it a great place for brunch, lunch, or dinner. Don't miss their fresh juices, smoothie bowls, and creative main courses that are as nutritious as they are tasty.

flaxandkale.com

L'Hortet

Catalan for 'little vegetable garden', this has been a beloved spot for over 25 years. Known for its daily changing lunch menu, L'Hortet offers options ranging from a full menu to a quick express meal with a dish and a dessert or coffee. On Fridays and Saturdays, the restaurant

takes on a trendier vibe in the evenings, featuring seasonal dishes like mushroom ravioli and homemade croquettes. The patatas bravas come with two delicious homemade sauces, and the highlight is the extensive, organic salad buffet.

Carrer de Pintor Fortuny 32, 08001 El Raval, restaurantvegetariahortet.com

Little Fern

A cosy café that offers a laid-back ambience. Specialising in creative plant-based dishes, Little Fern brings a unique twist to traditional brunch fare. Their menu features New Zealand-inspired plates fused with global culinary influences. Popular among the locals in the residential area of Poblenou, where this brunch place is located.

Carrer de Pere IV, 08005 Barcelona, littleferncafe.com

Maoz

Maoz is a casual fast-food spot that specialises in fresh, tasty falafel. Perfect for a quick and affordable meal, Maoz offers customisable pitas and salad bowls packed with fresh veggies, hummus, and their signature falafel. At the self-serve salad bar, you can choose your favourite toppings.

Carrer de Ferran 13, 08002 El Gòtic, maozfalafel.eu

Roots & Rolls

A haven for sushi lovers who prefer their rolls plant-based. This innovative restaurant combines traditional Japanese flavours with fresh, local ingredients to create unique vegan sushi and Asian fusion dishes. The chic minimalist decor makes it a cool spot for a laid-back meal with friends.

Carrer del Consell de Cent 401, 08009 L'Eixample, rootsandrolls.com

Rasoterra

This has been a beacon in Barcelona's green dining revolution since its opening in 2013. With a strong commitment to zerokilometre cuisine, Rasoterra sources ingredients from its own garden. The restaurant offers a gastronomic experience with sophisticated and tasty dishes. This dedication to quality, sustainability, and creativity makes it a must-visit if you're looking for an exceptional plant-based dining experience.

Carrer del Palau 5, 08002 Barcelona, rasoterra.cat

Sesamo

A no-nonsense vegetarian restaurant with a cosy, intimate atmosphere. On the menu, you can find a variety of international plates, from Indian curry to Italian pasta. Sesamo also offers a set vegetarian tapas menu, and a vegan option as well.

Carrer de Sant Antoni Abat 52, 08001 El Raval, insta @sesamobcn

Teresa Carles

A pioneer in Barcelona's vegetarian cuisine, blending traditional Catalan culinary influences with a focus on natural and healthy ingredients. With roots in the rural Catalan province Lleida, Teresa aims to create dishes as delicious as those made by both her grandmother and mother, but with a healthier twist. The result is tasty, healthy and sustainable.

Carrer de Jovellanos 2, 08001 Barcelona, teresacarles.com

The Green Spot

This is a chic, stylish restaurant that offers a creative and diverse plant-based menu. This spot is perfect for a night out with friends or a dinner date. Their dishes are beautifully presented with a focus on fresh, high-quality ingredients. The Green Spot is not the cheapest restaurant in town, but it does deliver a true dining experience.

Carrer de la Reina Cristina 12, 08003 La Barceloneta, grupotragaluz.com/restaurantes/the-green-spot

↓ LITTLE FERN

↓ FAIRE BRUNCH & DRINKS

Vegan Junk Food Bar

Indulge in your guilty pleasures without the guilt. Go to Vegan Junk Food Bar for delicious, plant-based versions of your favourite fast foods, from burgers and fries to 'chicken' wings. The colourful interior and creative dishes are perfect for some Insta-worthy shots. Located in both El Born and L'Eixample.

veganjunkfoodbar.com

Veggie Garden

Veggie Garden was one of the first vegetarian spots in Barcelona. Known for its affordable vegetarian and vegan dishes, this spot is a favourite among budget-conscious diners. Their menu is full of international flavours, from Indian rice platters to Mediterranean wraps, ensuring there's something for everyone.

veggiegardengroup.com

OUTSIDE OF BARCELONA

Barcelona offers endless adventures beyond the city limits. Whether you're looking to unwind by the beach, explore charming villages, or hike in the scenic mountains, the surrounding area has it all. In the warmer months, locals often head to the coast for a seaside escape. A visit to Montserrat is highly recommended for breathtaking views and hiking trails. Art lovers should not miss out on the Dalí heritage in Figueres. Many options are easily accessible by public transport. These are our favourites.

Sitges

visitsitges.com

Just a forty-minute train ride from Barcelona, Sitges is the perfect coastal escape. It's known for its beautiful beaches, vibrant nightlife, and charming old town. Spend your day soaking up the sun on the sandy shores, exploring the streets filled with boutique shops and cafés, or visiting the iconic Maricel Museum. Sitges is also famous for its LGBTQ+ friendly atmosphere and hosts an incredible Carnival every February.

Montserrat

visitsitges.com

A trip to Montserrat is a must for nature lovers and adventure seekers. Just an hour from Barcelona by train, this stunning mountain range is home to the Montserrat Monastery and offers breathtaking views over Catalonia.

↓ BLANES

The hike up to Sant Jeroni, the highest peak, is challenging but absolutely worth it. You'll be rewarded with panoramic views that stretch to the Pyrenees on a clear day. Culture lovers should not miss the opportunity to see the famous Black Madonna and listen to the boys' choir perform at the monastery.

Dalí Museum

Plaça Gala i Salvador Dalí 5, Figueres 17600 Figueres, salvador-dali.org

For art enthusiasts, a day trip to the eccentric Dalí Theatre-Museum in Figueres is an unforgettable experience. Just an hour-and-a-half train ride from Barcelona, this museum is a surreal masterpiece, designed by Salvador Dalí himself. You'll explore a vast collection of his works, including paintings, sculptures, and even his crypt. Combine your visit with a stroll around the charming town of Figueres. Visiting Dalí's birth house is highly recommended if you're interested in the artist's life.

Lloret-to-Blanes Hike

Escape the city and explore the beautiful Costa Brava coastline by hiking from Lloret de Mar to Blanes. This scenic trail, part of the GR-92 long-distance footpath, offers stunning views of rugged cliffs, hidden coves, and crystal-clear waters. The hike is relatively easy, making it perfect for all fitness levels. And it's easy to get there: take the train from Barcelona to Blanes (which takes roughly an hour and twenty minutes) and travel onward to Lloret by bus. You can catch the train back to the city from Blanes.

PortAventura World

portaventuraworld.com

For a day of thrills and fun, head to PortAventura World, located about an hour from Barcelona. This massive theme park complex includes PortAventura Park, Ferrari Land, and Caribe Aquatic Park. It's the largest theme park in Spain and offers a variety of rides and various adrenaline-pumping roller coasters. Experience the high-speed thrills of the Red Force roller coaster in Ferrari Land or cool off in the wave pools and water slides at Caribe Aquatic Park.

Penedès

penedesturisme.cat

Wine lovers will enjoy a trip to the Penedès region, famous for its production of cava, Catalonia's sparkling wine. Just a short train ride from Barcelona, this picturesque area is dotted with vineyards and wineries. Book a tour to visit some of the renowned wineries like Codorníu or Freixenet, where you can learn about the winemaking process and enjoy tastings of their exquisite cavas and wines.

↓ DALÍ MUSEUM

mmb
BARCELONA

INDEX

ABOUT THE AUTHORS

Antoinette Nelisse

In 2019, Antoinette, who is Dutch, moved to Barcelona to study for a year. She fell in love with the city and the rest is history. She has lived in the old town ever since the start of her Spanish adventure. She loves the international vibe, the beautiful parks and beaches and checking out new cafés.

Ruben Zuijderwijk

Ruben is a Dutch student who lived in Barcelona for several months during an internship. He believes the city offers the perfect mix of history, nightlife, delicious tapas, and beautiful weather. He plans to return to Barcelona in the future.

Annebeth Vis

Dutch journalist Annebeth has lived in Barcelona for over twenty years. She knows all the hidden gems – and where to find the best tapas. She has written dozens of articles and travel guides about the city. She organises walking and cycling tours and owns *barcelonatipsbylocals.com*.

WHY SHOULD I GO TO BARCELONA
the city you definitely need to
visit before you turn 30 (or 130)

Published in 2024 by mo'media
P.O. Box 359, 3000 AJ Rotterdam,
The Netherlands, momedia.nl

Concept
mo'media

Text and address selection
Annebeth Vis, Antoinette Nelisse, and
Ruben Zuijderwijk

Art direction and illustration design
Jelle F. Post

Editing
Ezra van Wilgenburg

Photography
Inez del Prado, Vincent van den
Hoogen, David in den Bosch, Eva van
den Berg, mo'media BV, and others

Special thanks to
Maaike van Steekelenburg

MIX
Paper from
responsible sources
FSC® C014138

WHY SHOULD I GO TO?
Information on all our travel guides
on **WHYSHOULDIGOTO.COM**

Why Should I Go To Barcelona
ISBN 978 94 9333 847 0
NUR 510

Disclaimer
The points of interested mentioned in this travel guide have been selected by the author. None of them have been paid for inclusion in this book: the *Why Should I Go To* book series is entirely ad-free.

Publisher's Note
Every effort has been made to ensure that the information in this book is accurate at the time of going to press. The publisher welcomes any information or suggestions for correction or improvement. Please send us an e-mail at info@momedia.nl or a DM on Instagram.

whyshouldigoto

Why Should I Go To travel guides are available for the following cities: Amsterdam, Antwerp, Barcelona, Berlin, Copenhagen, London, Paris, and Prague. More cities will be added soon. Check our socials for updates.